THE
CONTINENTAL DRAMA
OF TO-DAY

OUTLINES FOR ITS STUDY

SUGGESTIONS, QUESTIONS, BIOGRAPHIES, AND BIBLIOGRA-
PHIES FOR USE IN CONNECTION WITH THE STUDY
OF THE MORE IMPORTANT PLAYS

By

BARRETT H. CLARK

Second Edition, Revised

NEW YORK
HENRY HOLT AND COMPANY
1915

PREFACE

A growing demand on the part of clubs, reading circles, schools, colleges, and universities for definite and systematic guidance in the study of the modern movement in drama has led me to compile this Outline, in which are included plays of representative authors, from Ibsen to the present day.

Most of these plays have distinctive features of technique or characterization or theme, so that when the student has completed a study of the plays in connection with the Outline, he should have a very definite knowledge of the essentials of dramatic technique in general, and the modern movement in particular.

The comment that precedes each play is intended to give the reader a few suggestions as to the nature of the work, its importance, and to furnish him with a method of attack; supplementary to this comment are suggestions and questions intended to stimulate thought, discussion, and a careful reading of the play.

As the Outline deals only with those plays which have been translated into English and are easily obtainable, there must of necessity be many important omissions. In each case, however, practically all the plays of an author, whether they have been translated or not, are listed in the bibliographical notes.

It is not possible to classify satisfactorily the Modern Drama movement in definite groups or periods, for new work is constantly appearing and standards changing. I have therefore arranged the dramatists according to countries, and placed their work, in a general way, chronologically.

In making the bibliographies, I have referred from time to time to the various bulletins and compilations of the Drama League of America, and hereby acknowledge my indebtedness.

I have found it very difficult to get dates or records of American performances, and will welcome additional information or corrections from my readers. Nearly all the performances in German were at the little Irving Place Theatre in New York, which has done much for the modern drama.

B. H. C.

CONTENTS

CONTENTS

THE CONTINENTAL DRAMA
OF TO-DAY

WHAT CONSTITUTES A PLAY

What is a play? The question is a difficult one, for a definition should include every play that critics in the past have classed as such, as well as every production of the present age, the classification of which is still a matter of contention. As we survey the drama from Eschylus to Ibsen, certain definite types of literature stand out which by their form and content are called plays; dramatic periods have given birth and later final shape to plays, which have remained as unquestioned models until the inauguration of a new dramatic period. The three great dramatic poets of Greece—Eschylus, Sophocles, and Euripides—gave permanence to the form of drama for the age in which they lived, and Aristotle formulated the theory of that drama.* The Romans derived their inspiration from the Greeks and left the form essentially as they found it. The various movements following immediately upon the Renaissance were inspired mostly by Seneca, a Roman whose plays are at least externally Greek. In France, Corneille and Racine were the great classical dramatists; each accepted the

* See "The Poetics of Aristotle."

old laws of technique, adding little to them in regard to form; in Italy there was no attempt to
question the validity of the ancient formula: Al-
fieri's tragedies are patterned after those of an-
tiquity.   In Spain, Lope de Vega and Calderon
invented a sort of Romantic drama of their own,
which was not, however, to exert widespread influence beyond the borders of the Peninsula.   But
it was during the age of Elizabeth that the Romantic dramatists, who disregarded most of the
rules of classical scholars and none more so than
Shakspere, attained their highest excellence.
Two of the three Unities he threw to the winds,
and the third he used with the unconsciousness
of genius.   We have only to compare " Twelfth
Night " or " Hamlet " with " Edipus the King "
or " Prometheus Bound " to realize the gulf sep-
arating the ancient and modern method of con-
structing plays.   Shakspere, together with twenty
others, gave a more or less clearly defined form to
the drama of his age, and this form was widely
used as a model until the present time.   In fact,
nearly every English poet of the nineteenth century wrote poetic plays under the influence of
Shakspere.   In another realm, the so-called comedy of " manners,"—which aimed at the depiction
and ridicule of contemporaneous life, its customs,
manner, modes of thought and living,—the English
Restoration ushered in a new dramatic age, and for

nearly two centuries Congreve and Vanbrugh and Farquhar, and later Sheridan and Goldsmith continued to furnish models for comedies of manners. Similar movements in France and Germany and—in the eighteenth century, in Italy—each contributed to the dramatic form. Beaumarchais brought the Romantic and satirical comedy to its height in France, with " The Marriage of Figaro," Lessing and Schiller originated types in Germany in " Minna von Barnhelm " and " The Robbers," and Goldoni did much to deserve the title of the " Italian Molière." In the following century Augier and Dumas fils, Scribe and Sardou brought the old forms of comedy to a degree of perfection that has caused their plays to be termed *bien faites* —well-made. Scribe and Sardou, in developing the comedy of intrigue, or plot ; Augier and Dumas fils, in originating the " thesis " or " problem " play, still exert widespread influence. If these latter mentioned dramatists had not written, it is doubtful whether Ibsen could have brought the dramatic form to so high a degree of perfection as he did.

In each of these periods a clearly defined type stands forth as representative of the highest achievement of that age ; in many cases some critic has synthesized his ideas on the form—as Aristotle did—most typical of the age, and left it a criterion for future generations. We now link together Sophocles and Greek tragedy, Shakspere and the Romantic play—tragedy and comedy—Molière and the satirical comedy of manners, Ibsen and the social drama of the present time.

To-day we are in the midst of a dramatic period, the extent and importance of which is now impossible to determine. It is an age of production, of experimentation, of revolt against the accepted forms of the past, against its ideas and prejudices. One dramatist, like Tchekoff, writes a play of pure character; another, like Bernstein, one in which the situation is all-important. There is the " intellectual " drama of Bernard Shaw and Granville Barker, where the author uses the stage as a medium for the expression of ideas; the " thesis " drama and the play with a " purpose," of Brieux and Hervieu, where the dramatist makes use of the dramatic form for the advancement and proof of theories, for the correction and exposition of social wrongs; there is the poetic drama of Stephen Phillips and Rostand, reminiscent of Shakspere, in which the author seeks to tell a story in a beautiful manner, for its own sake and for the sake of the beauty of the language in which it is clothed. Is it possible, then, to speak of the age as Realistic, or Intellectual, or Romantic? Can we accurately apply any term to it as yet?

Obviously, no definition of the past can include

the mass of dramatic works which have during the
past twenty-five years made their appearance.   If
we apply the formula of the well-made play, we
eliminate Tchekoff and most of Shaw—to mention
no others; if we hold up Shakspere as a shining
example of the perfect dramatist, scarcely will a
living writer survive; if we revert to Aristotle, we
must rest content with "The Servant in the
House" and a few imitations of the ancients.

Can we approximate a new definition?   Mr.
Clayton Hamilton* says that "a play is a representation, by actors, on a stage, before an audience,
of a struggle between individual human wills, motivated by emotion rather than by intellect, and expressed in terms of objective action."   The great
majority of plays, past and present, fall easily
within the range of this admirable definition, and
yet the disquieting fact remains that it does not
cover a large number of works which will doubtless
take a permanent place in the drama when the history of this period is finally recorded.   A wider
definition, to be used at least as a working hypoth-
esis, must be found for the present.   This will be
discussed later on.

The prime difference between the dramatic and
other forms is that a play is a " representation, *by
actors, on a stage, before an audience.*"   It is perhaps an exaggeration to assert that a play which

* In "The Theory of the Theatre."   (Holt, 1910.)

is not performed is no play, but the parallel may legitimately be drawn between a picture that is not seen or a symphony that is not heard. A drama is written not to be read, but to " be played before an audience." This is its distinguishing feature. The fact that it must be presented before an audience materially limits its form and content. M. Gustave LeBon * tells us that when a crowd is gathered together for a common purpose, its collective self tends to lose the " mental qualities in which men differ from one another," and assumes " the qualities in which they are at one," which are the " innate passions of race." That is, a theater audience is emotional rather than intellectual. An individual in that audience, because he is a member of a crowd assembled for a common purpose, is more readily appealed to by a display of emotion than of intellect; Marguérite Gautier, in the play known in America as " Camille," is a more compelling figure than the " intellectual " Trebell in Mr. Barker's " Waste." When Shelley and Browning wrote plays they were not aware that they were writing for the individual, not for the collective body which went to the theater to feel, not primarily either to think or to listen to beautiful verse. There is something to be said in favor of the man who checks his brains with his overcoat.

* In " La Psychologie des Foules."

This is what Mr. Hamilton means when he says that a play must be " motivated by emotion rather than by intellect." But must a play be a " struggle between individual human wills "? The question is worth consideration. The French critic Brunetière * declares that "the theater in general is nothing but the place for the development of human will, attacking the obstacles opposed to it by destiny, fortune, or circumstance." This critic allows for possible exceptions by his inclusion of the word " general," and William Archer † has called attention to the fact that neither " As You Like It," nor " Ghosts," nor " Hannele " contains such a struggle. Maeterlinck's " The Blind," " The Intruder," and " Interior " may be mentioned as further examples of plays with no struggle, while " Œdipus the King " and " The Weavers " are, each in its way, devoid of any " struggle between conflicting individual human wills." " Œdipus " contains a struggle, but not " between conflicting individual human wills," while " The Weavers " is a struggle between conflicting wills of *bodies* of individuals, between employers and employed. I wish merely to point out that such a conflict as is spoken of in the definition, is not a necessary prerequisite. It is, however, one of the chief factors of interestingness,

* In " Etudes critiques," vol. vii., pp. 153 and 207.
† In " Playmaking." See page 95, present volume.

just as a struggle anywhere, in literature or life, is interesting. In the theater it has the additional advantage of appealing to the emotions rather than to the intellect.

The dramatist is further limited because the attention of his audience cannot safely be taxed for a greater period than two or two and a half hours. He must therefore lose no time in starting his story. A novelist may write one or many introductory chapters of preparation and explanation, and then begin his plot; a dramatist has only a few moments in which to explain and prepare. If by the end of half an hour he has not aroused the interest or enlisted the sympathy of his audience he will play to empty houses. And the reason, as M. LeBon has pointed out, is that whereas we are willing to sit in our library and read for many hours, in public, as part of a throng, we must feel, sympathize, see. On the stage a character must do, not be. We can see him do, we cannot see him think. Meredith may tell us in four or five hundred pages how Willoughby Patterne thinks, but Shakspere must show us in one-eighth the time the external results of Hamlet's mental state—even if at times he does furnish us with certain superb samples of his hero's intellectual power.

The last few years have brought forth numerous experiments in dramatic form, in Russia, Germany, and England. It is in attempting to place many of these under some distinct category that the student finds he has no adequate criterion of judgment. Is there a definition which can include works of so widely different character as Tchekoff's "Cherry Orchard," Wedekind's "The Awakening of Spring," Hauptmann's "Hannele," and Shaw's "Getting Married"? Tchekoff's play lacks unity, has little appeal to the emotions; Wedekind's is an inchoate series of realistic and madly romantic pictures, Hauptmann's is a "dream-poem" with no struggle, and Shaw's is a "discussion." And yet who shall say these are not plays?

Mr. Hamilton's definition * is one of the best yet formulated, but it must with the advance of time be widened. A play should of course be some sort of representation, usually a story, played by actors before an audience. This much is clear then, but as to subject-matter, we have observed, there is some question. Certainly a struggle is of great importance, but there are and always will be plays that are plays without it; nor need the struggle be between individual human wills. It is convenient and usually very dramatic to personify great social or political forces or "wills" in individuals, and such wills are usually found in individuals; but a body of individuals can likewise have a "will." Hauptmann has proved that.

Bearing in mind these few essentials, and accept-

* Which he has since considerably modified.

ing Mr. Hamilton's definition with the modifications made necessary by a number of recent successful innovators, we may inquire briefly into what constitutes a good play, and consider some method of approach and basis of judgment by which we may enjoy and criticise intelligently what we see in the theater—or read, as the case may be.

The theater is first and foremost and finally a place of amusement. It may teach, it may demonstrate, it may antagonize or disgust, but it must amuse. Perhaps the word amusement needs some explanation, for what amuses me may bore you, what edifies, interests, or pleases me, may send you packing after the first act. Amusement, then, in the broadest significance of the word may be assumed to mean the quality of pleasing, of appealing to our imagination pleasurably through the senses. "Edipus the King" has been acted and read for over two thousand years, yet it deals with patricide and incest; "Macbeth" is brutal and bloody, and yet is played and read in every part of the world. Both plays please, or they would not have survived. They are tragedies: they show great men struggling with forces which are greater than they and which finally dominate them. They appeal to the sympathies, to the imagination, and, because of their literary form, to the esthetic sense. They are, besides, interesting stories. They amuse. Both as it happens have " lessons " to teach, but that is merely because life has a lesson to teach; and the great artist in foreshortening and synthesizing and shaping his materials has brought that lesson of life into sharper relief and made it stand out in clearer terms than it does in the irrelevant and infinitely complex thing we call life. It is only when the dramatist sees his lesson or moral first and then tries to shape a semblance of life to fit it, that he fails to amuse. His lesson is repugnant to us, for it is obvious that the lesson's " the thing " and not the play. Sophocles and Shakspere and Molière wrote for the purpose of amusing, they happened to have the divine spark.

Underlying all art is the principle of unity, and the reason for this is a psychological one. When you look at an object your attention cannot remain fixed upon it for more than a few consecutive seconds, and while it is thus occupied there is but a " fringe of consciousness," as James terms it, giving attention to the objects immediately surrounding it. When you look at a Rembrandt portrait your attention is at once riveted upon one specific point, the head, let us say. The artist knows that if he puts in two points of equal or nearly equal interest the attention of the beholder will be divided: that his picture, in fine, will lack unity. The composer is aware that if he introduces a number of equally interesting themes, failing to reiterate and develop one which will stand out above the rest, he will cause a scattering of attention: that his composition will lack unity. Likewise the skilled dramatist knows that his story must be swift, compact, and essentially one, that his audience must be conducted as directly as is compatible with truth to life straight to the point of supreme interest and tension: the apex, the climax. He may insert a subordinate plot, or even two, but these must aid the central idea, and serve only as contrast or diversion. The play must hold the attention of the audience by its unity. Yet unity is not an end in itself, it is only a means, a psychological necessity. No play can succeed merely because it is unified. It is only when unity is joined with qualities of imagination and beauty, effectiveness and entertainment, that it is of use.

When you go to the theater, not with the idea of edifying yourself or learning, or judging, but for the sake of amusement, you ask only to be interested. If, after seeing the play you ask yourself why you were amused and interested, how will you be able to answer the question? Let us say that the story is good; assume that the play is "The School for Scandal." You enjoy the wit of the lines; they are clever, well phrased, and appropriate. They happen to be literature, but let us leave that question aside. Bright lines are not sufficient to carry a play. The story interests from the first; we like the intrigue, the working

out of human motives by means of human
agents. We enjoy Oliver's plan to find out
the attitude of Charles, we are excited in
the " screen " scene, we are anxious to learn the
outcome of Sir Peter and Lady Teazle's domestic
wrangles. Finally, we like the basic idea. We
dislike affectation and hypocrisy, and heartily
applaud any attempt to unmask the shallow pre-
tenses of our fellow-beings; we like nothing better
than to see virtue triumphant and baseness get its
just deserts. Further, most of us take pleasure in
seeing men and women like ourselves and observing,
with the aid of the dramatist's skill in characterization, how their minds work, and how they behave
under unusual circumstances. We take particular
pleasure in seeing them in embarrassing and painful situations—on the stage, at least. We take
keen delight in sympathizing with Ophelia, we are
excited and interested and moved when we see Lady
Macbeth wring her hands in despair. How many
of us are prompted to leave the theater at the beginning of the " sleep-walking " scene because we
cannot bear the suffering of the unfortunate lady?
In " The School for Scandal," then, are to be found
most of the elements of a good play: an interesting
and well-constructed plot, good characterization
and a good central idea, or theme.

How, precisely, does Sheridan bring about this
combination which in the form of a comedy has

given pleasure for so many years? By what process does the dramatist so arrange his material as to interest audiences, and perchance tell them something worth learning? This question it is the purpose of the present volume to consider, in suggesting to the student what is best and most representative in the drama of the present period.

A word of warning may be necessary: in the analysis of human handiwork, in the critical consideration of any work of art, the purpose of the artist must never be forgotten. That purpose is to give us pleasure. It cannot be too emphatically urged that a play is intended to amuse, not to furnish material for dissection.

HENRIK IBSEN

Henrik Ibsen was born March 20th, 1828, in Skien,
Norway. He spent a number of years at Grimstad as
apprentice to an apothecary, and in 1850 entered the
University of Christiania; soon after, he visited Co-
penhagen and Dresden for the purpose of making a
study of the stage, in preparation to his assuming the
managership of the theater of Bergen. He remained
in Bergen for five years, and at the end of that period
went to Christiania, to manage another theater. In
1862, he was forced to relinquish this theater and become " esthetic adviser " to still another theater.
Two years later he left Norway, and lived in Italy
and Germany until 1874, when he returned to his native land; after a short sojourn there, he returned to
Germany and lived in Dresden and Munich until 1891,
at which time he finally made his home in Christiania,
residing there until his death, in 1906.

Ibsen cannot be said to be a great originator, either
technically or philosophically. As a dramatist he
owes much to Augier and Dumas fils; as a philosopher to Schopenhauer and Nietzsche. He did, however, eventually develop a technique all his own and
a philosophy apart from that of any of his intellectual forbears. His great importance lies in the

17

fact that he took the " well-made " play where the
French had left it and brought it to a state of perfection which no one has as yet improved upon.
Like many philosophers he often changed his ideas ;
in " An Enemy of the People " Doctor Stockmann
asserts that most truths cease to be such after
twenty years' time ; in his poetic dramas and in
many of his social pieces he preaches the doctrine
of ideals, and in " The Wild Duck " he seems to
deny their value. Yet if his work is viewed in its
entirety, something like a philosophy of life, a distinct system of thinking and belief, may be traced.
Above all, Ibsen believed in the individual, in his
right to live his life in accordance with his personal
creed, in spite of all obstacles ; he says time and
again that a man in order to realize the best that
is in him must have the courage, the will, to be
himself. Now the individual who so wills invari-
ably finds the serried ranks of society against him ;
if he be strong enough he will break the social
bonds, if not, he is merely weak, and fails. Nora
must " live her life " ; she is forced, in order to do
this, to leave home and family, thereby shattering
one of the most " inviolable " shibboleths of society. Ibsen is determined to bring to judgment
most of the social prejudices of his time, and the
result is that for thirty years all the scorn and
hatred of an outraged social system are heaped
upon his head. The fearful and acrimonious at-

tacks made against him on the appearance of
"A Doll's House" and "Ghosts" were merely indications of the horror with which his ideas were
regarded by the people of the time, but the calm
acquiescence with which a much more outspoken
play than either of these—Brieux's "Damaged
Goods"—is now accepted gives ample proof that
society was only a few years behind the Scandinavian leader.

As a poet of prime importance, as an original
and in many ways revolutionary thinker, as dramatic craftsman and artist Ibsen is rightly considered the greatest of modern dramatists, and one
of the few dramatists of all time.

PLAYS

CATILINA (published 1850, produced 1881).

THE WARRIOR'S MOUND (produced 1850, published
1854).

OLAF LILJEKRANS (produced in a revised version
1857, published in German 1898).

LADY INGER AT OSTRAT (produced 1855, published
1857).

THE FEAST AT SOLHAUG (1856).*

THE VIKINGS AT HELGELAND (published 1858, produced 1861).

Produced at a single performance in 1907 by Sar-
gent's American Academy of Dramatic Arts.

* The date alone indicates the year of publication and
production.

LOVE's COMEDY (published 1862, produced 1873).

Produced at a few matinées in New York 1908.

THE PRETENDERS (1864).

Produced in New York and on tour by Yale Dramatic Association 1908.

BRAND (published 1866, produced in its entirety 1885).

Act IV given at New Theater, New York, 1910.

PEER GYNT (published 1867, produced 1876).

Produced by Richard Mansfield in the United States 1906.

THE LEAGUE OF YOUTH (1869).

EMPEROR AND GALILEAN (published 1873, produced in its entirety 1903).

THE PILLARS OF SOCIETY (published 1877, produced 1878).

Produced in New York in German 1889. In English 1889, and later by Mrs. Fiske 1910.

A DOLL's HOUSE (published 1879, produced 1880).

Produced in New York by Mrs. Fiske 1894; in German 1896-7.

GHOSTS (1881).

Produced in New York in English by Ida J. Goodfriend at a matinée 1895, and later by Mary Shaw; in German 1896-7.

AN ENEMY OF THE PEOPLE (published 1882, produced 1883).

Given single performances in New York by Beerbohm Tree 1895 and by Julius Hoppe's Progressive Stage Society 1905.

THE WILD DUCK (published 1884, produced 1885).

Produced in New York in German 1896-7.

ROSMERSHOLM (published 1886, produced 1887).

Produced in New York in English 1904, and by Mrs. Fiske 1908; in German 1897-8.

THE LADY FROM THE SEA (published 1888, produced 1889).

Produced in New York in German 1905-6; in English in Chicago and on tour by The Drama Players 1911.

HEDDA GABLER (published 1890, produced 1891).

Produced in New York in English by several noted actresses including Mrs. Fiske (1904) and Mme. Nazimova.

THE MASTER BUILDER (published 1892, produced 1893).

Produced in New York in Russian, and in English by Nazimova 1907.

LITTLE EYOLF (published 1894, produced 1895).

Though it had occasional single performances (one in 1907-8) earlier, the first important one was by Nazimova in 1910.

JOHN GABRIEL BORKMAN (published 1894, produced 1897). In New York, matinée 1897.

WHEN WE DEAD AWAKEN (published 1899, produced 1900).

Produced in New York 1905.

Mention is made in the books of Brandes, Moses, and Heller, of " St. John's Eve," " The Lonely One," " Norma; or, A Politician's Love," and a fragment, " The Grouse of Justedal; a National Play in Four Acts." These unimportant items complete the list of Ibsen's plays. Of the above, " Catilina," " The Warrior's Mound," " Olaf Liljekrans," and the four plays just mentioned have not been translated into English; " Catilina," " The Warrior's Mound," and " Olaf Lil- jekrans " are published in French, in the translation of MM. de Colleville and de Zepelin. The best and only collected edition of the plays of Ibsen in English is that edited by William Archer, and published in the United States by Scribner. A translation of " Peer Gynt " in the original meter by R. Ellis Rob- erts is announced by Kennerley.

The following are some of the more important ref- erence books on Ibsen:

Henrik Jaeger: " Henrik Ibsen: A Critical Biogra- phy." McClurg, 1890.

H. H. Boyesen: " A Commentary on the Writings of Ibsen." Macmillan.

Georg Brandes: " Henrik Ibsen—Björnstjerne Björnson." Macmillan.

Philip H. Wicksteed: " Four Lectures on Henrik Ibsen." Sonnenschein.

Edmund Gosse: " Henrik Ibsen." Scribner.

Haldane McFall: " Ibsen: The Man, His Art, and His Significance." Morgan, Shepard.

George Bernard Shaw: " The Quintessence of Ib- senism." Brentano. Revised edition 1913.

Montrose J. Moses: " Henrik Ibsen: The Man and His Plays." Kennerley.

Otto Heller: " Henrik Ibsen, Plays and Problems." Houghton Mifflin.

Jennette Lee: " The Ibsen Secret." Putnam.

The introductions of Archer to the individual plays in the Collected Edition should also be consulted, as well as the volume entitled " From Ibsen's Workshop," which contains a number of Ibsen's scenarios and preliminary sketches. The "Letters of Henrik Ibsen," published by Duffield, and the "Speeches and New Letters of Henrik Ibsen," published by Badger, are also of value.

THE PRETENDERS

A historical drama in five acts. First published 1864. (In Volume II, Ibsen's Collected Works. Scribner.)

Although the play is founded upon incidents taken from early history, and the main facts in it are authentic, much has been added by the poet; chiefly the motivation of the leading characters. "The Pretenders" is a considerable advance over "The Vikings," the historical play that preceded it; the characters are more strikingly individual, the story as well told, yet more intricate. Because of its essentially dramatic form, its subject-matter, and its literary style, the play is by some critics considered Ibsen's finest dramatic achievement.

This play is concerned primarily with the characters of Skule and Hakon: Skule, the king by actual right, Hakon the king "by confidence." The author has taken an old story and put a distinctly modern theme into it. Bishop Nicholas says to Skule, "The right is his [Hakon's], for he is the fortunate one; 'tis even the summit of fortune, to have the right. But by what right has Hakon the right, and not you?" This is the central idea of the play.

1. Observe how the "atmosphere" is created in the opening scene. The setting, the crowds in the street, the incident of the ordeal, all combine to give the spirit in which the action is to take place.

2. As in practically all plays, a scene of less tension follows one of storm and stress; note how the scene between Lady Ragnhild and Margrete releases the tension created by the preceding one. Note, too, how the conversation between these two contains a good deal of exposition. This colloquy gives the audience what information it is necessary they should know in order to understand what is happening, or going to happen.*

Notice how scenes are contrasted throughout the play.

3. The scene just referred to—that between Lady Ragnhild and Margrete—contains a good deal of repetition (see pp. 132-133). This is done in order that the audience may not miss an important point. Scribe is said to have repeated all his important points three times, and it is safe to say that all successful playwrights have acted on the principle that to state a fact once is not sufficient.—Another good example of this is found throughout Sir Arthur Pinero's "The Thunderbolt."

4. Most plays do not actually begin the moment

* See Archer's "Playmaking," chapter on Exposition.

the curtain rises; time is necessary to introduce
the chief characters and tell something of the past.
In nearly every play it is easy to detect just where
the action begins. Where in " The Pretenders "
does exposition stop and the story, or action,
begin?

5. One of the commonly observed " laws " of
playwriting is, Never keep a secret long from the
audience. A usual method to this end is to drop
hints early in the play as to what is going to occur.
In Pinero's " Mid-Channel " Zoe Blundell says,
" You'll see, when I put an end to myself, it will
be in the winter time." In Galsworthy's " Justice "
Falder says to Ruth, " It *is* too late " [to stay,
i. e.]. These are examples of foreshadowing, or
giving the audience some inkling of what is to
happen later. Bishop Nicholas, in " The Pretenders," says, " Ever on your guard, good Dagfinn—
ever on your guard."—Find other examples of
foreshadowing in the present play.

6. It is the function of every first act—and of
every other save the last—to throw out some hint
of what is to follow in the next; very few acts can
stand independently and give no clue to the story
to come. It is usually toward the end of the act
that such indications are found. They are in the
nature of a " Continued in our next," and serve as
binding links in the story.

At the end of the second act of Björnson's " The

Gauntlet " (First Version, Everyman's Library),
Christenson says, " Then it is to be war?—Well, I
fancy I know a thing or two about war," and goes
out. That speech and the manner in which it is
delivered, arouse the interest of the audience, so
that they eagerly await the next act. Another
good example is at the end of the first act of
Wilde's "Lady Windermere's Fan," where Lady
Windermere declares her intention of striking Mrs.
Erlynne over the face if she comes to the reception.
In " The Pretenders," Hakon says, " At last, then,
I am King of Norway," and Earl Skule replies,
" But I rule the realm." If it were not for this
disquieting remark, the first act might almost stand
as a complete one-act-play.

7. Find the " bridging-over " sections in the subsequent acts.

BRAND

A play in five acts. First published 1866.
(In Volume III, Ibsen's Collected Works.)

" Brand " is a dramatic poem in five acts. It was
not written originally for the stage, but it has been
produced with considerable success in most of the
countries of Europe.

The play is concerned with a man who sacrifices
everything to his ideal of " All or nothing "; Brand
gives up friends, wife, and child, for his principles.
Technically, the plot is well constructed and interest-

ing as a story; as a play, it is doubtful whether the long speeches add to its general effectiveness.

1. Notice again the setting. The key-note of the play is to be found there. A good dramatist rarely gives the audience a false clue in his opening act; either by setting, conversation, or pantomime, or all three, he foreshadows as it were the spirit of the play.—Compare the opening of " Brand " with those of " Macbeth " and " Hamlet."

2. At precisely what point does " Brand " start? That is, where does the introduction, or exposition, stop, and the plot begin?

3. What examples of foreshadowing are there in the first act? Where, in the first act, is there a connecting link of interest, carrying the story into the succeeding act?

4. After the introduction, or exposition, which is always in the first act, and after the play starts,* that section of the play which is known as the development, begins. This extends to the climax, the high-water mark of interest—the " greatest of a series of crises," the point from which the play releases its tension and falls, to the conclusion. In Sudermann's " Magda," practically the entire first act is devoted to exposition; not until the very last part of it does the play start. The moment

* Archer calls this setting in motion of the wheels of the play, " joining the issue." See " Playmaking."

Schwartze says he will let his daughter come to see him the play has begun.—By way of comparison trace carefully the development of " Brand," noting where the exposition stops, where the action begins, and where it reaches its culmination.

5. Every scene, in its action and in what it contains of characterization, contributes to the exposition of various sides of Brand's nature. This adherence to one personage, continuous and yet interesting in its variations, makes for unity, both of the play and of the character of the protagonist. When the play is read, a distinct and unified impression remains, in spite of many scenes and seemingly countless incidents.

6. What is the dramatic, or structural, purpose of the Dean, the Mayor, and of Einar?

NOTE.—For information on the meaning and symbolism of " Brand," see Moses' " Ibsen," and Jennette Lee's " The Ibsen Secret."

PEER GYNT

A play in five acts.　First published 1867.
(In Volume IV, Ibsen's Collected Works.)

" Peer Gynt " may be taken as complementary to " Brand." In the former play, the hero is a man of indomitable will; in the latter, he is a man almost without it. In " Peer Gynt," Ibsen satirized the weak-

nesses of the Norwegian people, incorporating them
into the character of Peer. Although at first the
play may seem disjointed and chaotic, the hero always
stands out clearly and one is left with a unified impression of the work as a whole.

1. Certain themes recur constantly in Ibsen's
plays, and one of the commonest is heredity.
Worked out finally in " Ghosts," it is to be found in
" A Doll's House " and " Peer Gynt." Peer owes
much in his character to his mother and a great
deal to his father; this we learn from Ase herself in
one of her early conversations with her son. How
great a factor heredity is when used for purposes
of motivation in a play, is an interesting study.
How far is Peer responsible for what he does?
How far is Nora Helmer? As for Oswald in
" Ghosts," it is safe to assert that Ibsen intended
him to be entirely blameless.

2. Ibsen's later plays—from " A Doll's House "
to " Hedda Gabler "—are often cited as models
of technical economy. And so they are, but it
must not be forgotten that the early plays are for
the most part admirable examples of the craftsman's skill. Read the first eleven pages of " Peer
Gynt " (in the edition cited) and notice how much
ground is covered: (a) the atmosphere is created;
the " wooded hillside," with the water rushing down
the slope, the old mill shed, serve to give the " milieu " or environment in which the action is to pass;

(b) the chief personage is introduced, and his dominant characteristics made apparent; (c) nearly all of the past that is necessary for the understanding of the play is made known; and, (d) some inkling as to Peer's fate is hinted at. These preliminaries are so skilfully introduced, so unobtrusively insinuated, that the reader scarcely realizes he has learned anything. Compare with this the opening pages of "Hedda Gabler," where the exposition is much more compact, almost too much so; in that play it is doubtful whether the audience could assimilate all that is set before it, because practically every word is full of import. In "Peer Gynt" there is sufficient matter of extraneous interest— such as the intrinsic beauty of the lines and the situation itself—to attract the reader or auditor, so that he will pay strict attention to all that is said and done. In the exposition of "Hedda Gabler" what actually happens is of comparatively little interest. Take any play, read the first five pages, and see how much the author has told, noting carefully whether it is attractively served, as it were, or merely lumped together.

3. Read "Peer Gynt" through as a story, a poem, a fantasy; the first time do not seek the full explanation of hidden meanings and symbols. The work is a satire on human nature, and if in places it is obscure, try to enter into its spirit, which is everywhere manifest. It is, of course, helpful to

know what the Boyg and the Button Moulder stand for, but not absolutely necessary.*

4. Compare the exposition of " Peer Gynt " with that of " The Pretenders " and " Brand." Compare the characters of Agnes and Solveig; what is the function of each, in relation to the chief character in the respective plays?

5. " Peer Gynt " is not a " well-made " play; it is not modeled upon any accepted formula, yet it is effective both as poetry and drama. Ibsen declared that if critics objected to his play on the ground that it was not poetry, they would have to change their conception of poetry to fit what he had written. Likewise may it not be urged that they who condemn " Peer Gynt " regarding it merely as a poem and no play must change their conception of what constitutes a play?

A DOLL'S HOUSE

A play in four acts. First published 1879.
(In Volume VII, Ibsen's Collected Works.)

Ibsen's so-called " social dramas," written between 1867 and 1899, differ widely in spirit and style from the works that have just been considered. Most of them consist of the end of a story, most of the events of which have happened long ago, and have

* See Archer's introduction to the Scribner edition; also chapters on " Peer Gynt " in the books of Moses and Heller.

been aptly called " catastrophic " plays, because they
deal almost exclusively with the end or catastrophe.
" Ghosts " is perhaps the best example.   When the
curtain rises on that play, everything but the inevitable result has taken place.   Ibsen is interested and
actually concerned only with the end.   " Ghosts " is
the dramatization of an effect;the cause of the tragedy
is over years before the play begins.   " A Doll's
House " is similar, because the audience sees only the
last part of the story.

The gist of the play is in the last half of the last
act, in the conversation between Nora and Helmer.
Ibsen once said that the play was written for the
sake of this scene.   The first three acts and the
first part of the fourth are preparation.   The exposition in the first act, the unfolding of Nora's
previous history, serve as additional preparation.
Therefore, when the momentous conversation takes
place, the audience has firmly in mind the important events in the lives of the characters.

Technically, this play is one of Ibsen's best; it
is clear, interesting, unified.   No time is lost in letting the audience know what has gone before.   We
are curious to know more, to learn how Nora will
extricate herself from her difficulties.   Throughout the play, there is scarcely a superfluous word:
all tends toward the final scene, all is virtually
preparatory explanation.

In studying this play—and, for that matter, all

plays—it will be well to reconstruct the story of what has happened previously to the rise of the curtain.

1. How does the conversation between Nora and Mrs. Linden advance the story in the first act? In other words, what is the purpose of Mrs. Linden in that act?

2. It has been said that every line in a good play does one of two things, if not both: advance the plot or reveal character. What is the purpose of the scene between Rank, Nora, and Mrs. Linden in the first act? What is the purpose of the scene with the children?

3. Do you see a good reason why Helmer should speak of Krogstad before his wife in the first act rather than in a later one, or why he should speak of his dealings with Krogstad at all?

4. Near the beginning of the second act, Nora says to the maid who tells her that if she goes out she may catch cold: "Worse things might happen." Is this a good example of foreshadowing? In the first two acts, are there any better examples? What are they?

5. What structural purpose is served by Rank's exposition of his views on heredity?

6. The play has sometimes been criticized on the ground that it was impossible for Nora to develop to so abnormal a degree within the three days allowed her by the author. Trace the steps by

which that development has progressed, and try to determine whether Ibsen has justified such a change.

Read the scene between Nora and Helmer in the last act and notice how, during the preceding acts, the scene is prepared for. Nora's acute reasoning power should not come as too great a surprise, for an audience has a right to be prepared for what is the outgrowth of the early part of the play.

HEDDA GABLER

A play in four acts. First published 1890.
(In Volume X, Ibsen's Collected Works.)

"Hedda Gabler" is one of the finest examples of dramatic technique in existence. As a study in construction it repays many readings and much careful application. The play deals with the character of a woman out of harmony with her surroundings. All the skill of the dramatist is brought to bear upon a complete revelation of her past life, her thoughts, and the resultant acts. Everything in the play contributes to the psychological portrait of Hedda Gabler.

1. The exposition is so deftly contrived that every word counts; in fact, the words "I don't believe they are stirring" arouse curiosity, give some past history, and afford some indication as to the character of the speaker. The first two pages

are so full of meaning that the reader—and certainly the auditor—must pay the strictest attention, or else lose important information. Up to George's entrance, we learn enough about him so that no time need be lost learning his further characteristics from himself. The presence of George varies the scene a little, and by the time the audience has seen him, it is ready for more information. Judge Brack is mentioned, then a little further action is introduced; farther on there is more exposition—telling us of the relations between Hedda and Miss Tesman. Little by little the details are piled up, until we know nearly all that is needful for a full comprehension of the remainder of the play.—Then Hedda makes her appearance.

Trace the steps in the introduction, and notice how the past gradually rises up and takes shape as background; how the characters are introduced, how each important detail is insisted upon, preparatory to the action that is to take place. The " curtain " of the first act closes the exposition, and the development begins.

2. The second act starts and advances the plot up to the climax. The climax is that point at which the action of the play reaches its culmination, the last stage in its development, from which the action falls, or is unraveled. In Henry Arthur Jones's " The Liars," Lady Jessica says to

Falkner (Act III), "Tell my husband the truth," and Falkner does so. That is the climax of the play; up to that point, the fortunes of most of the people depended upon a network of lies, and when these are discovered and the truth learned, tension is released, and the only thing to wait for is the explanation. The rest of the play shows merely the result of the revelation. In "Hedda Gabler," the climax is Hedda's burning of the "child," Lövborg's MS.; that deed is the culminating point of those events, or crises, in her life with which Ibsen, either in the play or before it, is concerned. From that point onward, we see only effects; never again does the action rise to so high a pitch. Hedda's death, even, is only the logical outcome of what has gone before, and that was prepared for, foreshadowed, in the first and succeeding acts.

NOTE.—"Hedda Gabler" is carefully analyzed in Charles H. Caffin's "Appreciation of the Drama." Ibsen's scenarios and sketches for this play are especially interesting, and are found in the volume entitled "From Ibsen's Workshop."

THE MASTER BUILDER

A play in three acts. First published 1892.
(In Volume X, Ibsen's Collected Works.)

"The Master Builder" marks the beginning of Ibsen's "third and last period." The historical and

poetical plays compose the " first period," and the
prose " social " dramas,—from " The League of
Youth " to " Hedda Gabler,"—the " second period."
In " The Master Builder " Ibsen is within the realm of
fancy; symbols are used to suggest more or less hidden truths, while the action itself must be considered
as unreal.   The tone of the play is poetical, although
the medium of expression is prose.   In order to understand the play better, which is to a great extent autobiographical, a certain incident should be known.
The following passage from Gosse's " Henrik Ibsen "
gives an interesting clue: " In the season of 1889,
among the summer boarders at Gossensass, there appeared a young Viennese lady of eighteen, Miss Emi-
lie Bardach.   She used to sit on a certain bench in the
Pferchthal, and when the poet, whom she adored from
afar, passed by, she had the courage to smile at him.
Strange to say, her smile was returned and soon Ibsen
was on the bench at her side.   He readily discovered
where she lived; no less readily he gained an introduction to the family with whom she boarded. . . .
Perhaps, until they parted in the last days of September, neither the old man nor the young girl realized
what their relations had meant to each.   Youth secured its revenge, however; Miss Bardach soon wrote
from Vienna that she was now tranquil, more independent, happy at last.   Ibsen, on the other hand, was
heart-broken, quivering with ecstasy, overwhelmed
with joy and despair."—Bearing in mind that " The
Master Builder " grew out of this incident, the play
is easier to understand.

1. Why should symbols be used in plays? Does their use in " The Master Builder," for instance, make the meaning clearer? Do such obvious symbols as those in Maeterlinck's " Blue Bird " help the reader or auditor?

2. Although "The Master Builder" is a considerable departure from the manner of the earlier plays, the main technical points, such as development, climax, etc., are still clearly discernible. Find these points and compare each section with those of "Hedda Gabler" and "A Doll's House."

3. Taking Solness as the embodiment of the older generation, and Hilda of the younger, and accepting the climbing of the tower as a symbol of aspiration, does the rest of the play follow logically? That is, granting the symbolic medium of expression, is the rest of the play comprehensible?

4. Do you think that "The Master Builder" would be more effective on the stage than if read? Later in the present volume, the question of whether some plays are injured by stage production and are better read than seen, is considered. Is "The Master Builder" one of these?

BJÖRNSTJERNE BJÖRNSON

Björnson, together with Ibsen the first Norwegian
to embody to any considerable extent the true spirit
of his native land in modern times and create a distinctly national literature, was born in Kvikne, Norway, in 1832. His primary education was received in
Molde. At the age of twenty, he entered the University of Christiania, where he made the acquaintance
of Ibsen. His first book appeared in 1857, an idyllic
novel, called " Synnöve Solbakken," which was received with considerable enthusiasm; it has remained
one of his most popular books. The following year
Björnson assumed the directorship of the Bergen
theater and there produced some of his earlier plays,
the subject-matter of which was drawn largely from
the Norse sagas. The next few years were devoted to
travel, the writing of stories, plays, and poems, and to
practical politics. The years 1865-1867 saw him in
charge of a theater in Christiania, as well as editor
of a newspaper, which he used to further his struggle
for Norwegian independence, political and literary.
For practically the rest of his life, Björnson participated in the great political upheaval in Norway, and
was considered the leader of the liberal party. In
1880 he came to America and delivered a number of
lectures in the Northwest. From 1881, when he returned to his native country, until 1910, when he died

in Paris, he spent most of his time on his estate in the south of Norway.

Although he was primarily a novelist and poet, Björnson claims a place among the foremost of modern dramatists, because he was the first to found the new drama in Norway, and among the first to employ that medium for a free discussion of individual rights and personal liberty, moral and intellectual.

PLAYS

BETWEEN THE BATTLES (1858).

LAME HULDA (1858).

KING SVERRE (1861).

SIGURD SLEMBE (1862). Part II produced by Donald Robertson, Chicago 1908.

MARY STUART (1864).

THE NEWLY-MARRIED COUPLE (1865). New York 1905 by American Academy of Dramatic Arts.

SIGURD JORSALFAR (1872).

THE EDITOR (1874).

A BANKRUPTCY (1874).   Academy of Dramatic Arts,

THE KING (1877).   [New York 1900.

LEONARDA (1879).

THE NEW SYSTEM (1879,.

A GAUNTLET (1883). By Robertson, Chicago 1907.

BEYOND OUR POWER, Part I (1883).

In United States by Mrs. Patrick Campbell 1902.
Produced in New York by Julius Hoppe's Progressive Stage Society 1905.

PAUL LANGE AND TORA PARSBERG (1898).

LABOREMUS (1901).
AT STORHOVE (1904).
DAGLARMET (1904).
WHEN THE NEW WINE BLOOMS (1909).

" Sigurd Slembe " is translated by William Morton
Payne (Sergel, Chicago, 1910); " Mary, Queen of
Scots " by Aug. Sahlberg (Specialty Syndicate Press,
Chicago, 1912); " The Newly-Married Couple " by R.
Farquharson Sharp (Everyman's Library, Dutton,
1913), and by G. T. Colborn (Brandu, New York,
1911) as " A Lesson in Marriage "; " Leonarda " in
The Drama, 1912, and by R. F. Sharp (Everyman's
Library, Dutton, 1913); " The New System " by Ed-
win Björkman (Scribner, 1913); " A Gauntlet " by
H. L. Braekstad, 1890, by Osman Edwards, 1894,
and in *The Drama,* vol. xvii (The Athenian So-
ciety, London), by R. F. Sharp (Everyman's Li-
brary, Dutton, 1913), and by Edwin Björkman
(Scribner, 1913); " Beyond Our Power," Part I, by
Edwin Björkman (Scribner, 1913); " Geography
and Love " by Edwin Björkman (Scribner, 1914);
" Beyond Our Power," Part II, by Edwin Björkman
(Scribner, 1914); " Laboremus " by Edwin Björkman (Scribner, 1914); " When the New Wine
Blooms " by Lee M. Hollander (*Poet-Lore*).

REFERENCES: Georg Brandes, "Henrik Ibsen—
Björnstjerne Björnson: Critical Studies " (Macmil-
lan); H. H. Boyesen, " Essays on Scandinavian Lit-
erature " (Scribner); William Morton Payne,
" Björnstjerne Björnson " (McClurg, Chicago).
Shorter essays and criticisms: See introductions to

"Sigurd Slembe" (Sergel); "Three Comedies of Björnsterne Björnson" (Everyman's Library); "Plays by Björnson," 1st Series: "The New System," "The Gauntlet," "Beyond Our Power," with introduction by Edwin Björkman—2d Series: "Love and Geography," "Beyond Human Might" ("Beyond Our Power," Part II), "Laboremus," with introduction by Edwin Björkman (Scribner); also Ashley Dukes, "Modern Dramatists" (Sergel, 1912); Edwin Björkman, "Voices of To-morrow" (Kennerley, 1913).

LEONARDA

A play in four acts. Originally published 1879. Translations in *The Drama,* and in Everyman's Library.

"Leonarda" is one of the first plays in the modern movement to treat of the "woman with a past." The author endeavors to show that such women as the heroine are capable of great sacrifice and ought not to be regarded as social outcasts. Society's attitude to such women is the subject, or theme, of the play; note that society's attitude toward men "with a past" is the theme, or a part of it, of "A Gauntlet."

1. Contrary to modern custom, the heroine appears on the stage at the rise of the curtain; in this way we enter immediately into the subject of the play. One side of Leonarda's character is quickly revealed: her sympathetic nature. The

attention of the audience is at once attracted by
movement and variety, and is not taxed by lengthy
exposition. A minute passes before this begins,
and when General Rosen inquires about Aagot the
audience is prepared to listen with interest. This
method of attracting attention and holding interest from the very beginning is not uncommon:
the opening scenes of "The Tempest" and
"Romeo and Juliet" are good examples of the
principle.

2. Good exposition, we have observed, is that
which seems natural and at the same time gives
valuable information while not appearing to do so.
The first scene between Hagbart and Leonarda is
good exposition, because the latter's questioning
of Hagbart gives us full details, and the important
points on an essential bit of past history; shows
Leonarda's relations with and attitude toward
Hagbart, and their feeling in turn for Aagot—
and all with perfect naturalness. The entire scene
is not only lifelike, it seems inevitable.

3. Generally speaking, the climax—the highest
point of dramatic interest—in a play occurs some-
where near the end of the penultimate act.*   It is

* Two interesting exceptions are "King Lear," where the
technical climax occurs at the very beginning of the play,
and William Vaughn Moody's "The Great Divide," in
which the climax is in the middle of the first act. The
latter author has difficulty in sustaining interest during
the rest of the play.

the point from which the action, and consequently
the suspense, descends, and the last act takes up
the concluding threads of the story, explains what
has gone before, and ends the play. In " Leonarda," the climax is where the chief character gives up Hagbart in favor of Aagot
(p. 94, Everyman's edition). The remainder of the act merely demonstrates the
immediate result of this renunciation, and
the fourth concludes the story in the shortest
possible way. For further illustration of the position and function of the climax, see the third
acts of Henry Arthur Jones's "The Liars," Oscar
Wilde's "Lady Windermere's Fan," and Sir
Arthur Pinero's " Iris."

A GAUNTLET

A play in three acts. Published 1883. Translations
listed above. Recommended texts: in Everyman's
Library, and in "Three Plays by Björnson"
(Scribner). The play was re-written in 1892.

" A Gauntlet " * is one of the most clearly defined examples of the thesis play. The author
wishes to show that a woman has the right to demand the same prenuptial chastity from her fiancé
as he demands of her ; it is a plea for the abolition

* This discussion is based upon the original version, as
the revised is not easily accessible.

of the " double standard." The fault with most
thesis plays is that the thesis occupies too prom-
inent a place, and that violence is done to the plot
and characters, owing to the fact that the author
must first of all establish and prove his case, at the
expense of verisimilitude. " A Gauntlet " is open
to this criticism. If a dramatist wishes to make
his play prove something, he should conceal any
conscious effort in so doing, and " bury his tools "
when through with them. This is precisely what
Brieux has done in his finest thesis play, " The Red
Robe." The evils incident to obtaining advancement in the French courts are what the French
dramatist wishes to expose, but his crushing indictment is not fully realized until after the close of
the play, for everything happens so naturally that
the attention of the audience is not distracted from
the story and the people who are so intimately
bound up in it. The thesis grows gradually and
inevitably out of the action, and this does not seem
to be merely a means, but an end in itself.

1. The " Gauntlet," being written primarily for
the sake of the " lesson," is unlike the Ibsen plays
we have considered. Ibsen always put into his
writings an idea, but rarely does he allow us to see
that he wrote a play for the idea itself. In " A
Gauntlet " everything points toward and supports
the central idea, every scene stands independently
as some phase of the theme, or else prepares the

way for such a scene. Bear these facts in mind as
you read the play, and judge of its effectiveness,
both as a piece of dramatic art and a thesis play.

2. A consideration of this work is rendered
doubly interesting if the two versions * are compared. The second act, as it was originally written, ends with Svava's throwing of the glove in
Alf's face, and Christensen's declaration of war.
This climax is good, and it occurs where we might
expect it to occur: at the end of the last act but
one. The last act has to do with the result of
Svava's challenge, and ends with her reconciliation with Alf. This seems fairly reasonable and
human, but Björnson's thesis suffers: if he wished
to preach the doctrine of the single standard, he
has weakened his argument by making his strong
character destroy it. Feeling that this was a
weakness, Björnson re-wrote the play, and made
his thesis stronger; he closes the second act with
Svava's enlightenment regarding her father's relations with Mrs. North. This is a sufficiently
dramatic climax in itself, but in that it creates
greater tension—because it leaves the outcome
more doubtful—than the first version, it is superior. The last act, therefore, of the new version is much better than that of the old, as the

* The revised version is in *The Drama,* vol. xvii (Athenian
Society, London); it is also in a French translation, published by P.-V. Stock, Paris, as " Un Gant."

audience eagerly awaits the " big scene " between
Svava and Alf. The throwing of the gauntlet
constitutes the end of the play, and we are no
longer in doubt as to Svava's feelings and the
author's ultimate intention. Now the climax of
the earlier play serves as the catastrophe*—so
called—of the later. But notice a still more unusual feature: while the climax is effective in both
versions, that of the first is the more so, but the
catastrophe is comparatively weak; the climax in
the second is adequate, and the catastrophe powerful and wholly convincing. As a rule, it is more
difficult to sustain interest in the last act than in
any other, so that, dramaturgically, the second
version of this play is incomparably better than
the original.

* The " Catastrophe " is the outcome, the final chord, the
result, of the play. The term is applicable to both tragedy
and comedy.

LEO TOLSTOY

Leo Tolstoy was born August 28, 1828, at Yasnaya Polyana, Russia. Soon after the early death of his parents he was sent in turn to live with his two aunts, the second of whom exerted an influence—as Tolstoy was only eleven years old—which was far from good. Four years later he entered the University of Kazan, and subsequently studied in the School of Eastern Languages and the law school. In 1847 he left the law school, tired of the life of comparative idleness and dissipation which he was then leading. After spending a few months at his home, he went to St. Petersburg with his brother, " carousing with Zigani dancers, and throwing all serious thoughts to the winds." In 1851 he joined the army in the Caucasus, whence he began sending back vivid accounts of the battles in which he participated. The Czar was soon attracted by the " Tales from Sebastopol," and had Tolstoy brought back to the capital. In 1857 he left his native country to travel in Germany, France, Italy, Switzerland, England, returning from time to time to Russia. In 1861 he was once more at Yasnaya Polyana; the next year he was married. The remainder of his life was devoted to the consideration of many political questions of the day, upon which he wrote numerous tracts; besides these, he published novels,

stories, longer political and philosophical works and
plays. For political and religious reasons he was in
1901 excommunicated from the Orthodox Church. He
died nine years later at Astapovo.

Tolstoy's best work is not in his plays, but there
is much good in them in spite of occasional scenes of
brutal and revolting realism. Nor is he great among
Russian dramatists; most of the Russians to be considered later are better craftsmen. But the development of the drama has been everywhere so rapid,
that it is interesting to study a comparatively early example of modern Russian drama. Tolstoy wrote his
plays for special and private performances, and their
technical requirements were not such as would be
made in the case of plays intended for professional
production. Tolstoy shares with other dramatists of
his country their lack of the sense of form; either they
have not yet learned the art of play-building or else
they have purposely avoided what they considered the
" tricks of the trade," preferring to lay greater stress
on the delineation of character. Whatever the reason,
the plays of Tolstoy, Tchckoff, Gorky, and Andreyeff are interesting primarily as revealing their authors' insight into humanity at large.

PLAYS

THE NIHILIST (1863).
THE INFECTED FAMILY (1864).
THE POWER OF DARKNESS (1886).
    In English by American Academy 1900. A few
      performances given in German, New York 1903.

THE FIRST DISTILLER (1887).

THE FRUITS OF CULTURE (1889).

Played in United States on tour by Yale Dramatic Association 1913.

THE MAN WHO WAS DEAD (1912).

THE LIGHT THAT SHINES IN DARKNESS (1912).

THE CAUSE OF IT ALL (1912).

" The Power of Darkness," " The First Distiller," and " The Fruits of Culture " are translated by Louise and Aylmer Maude in " Plays by Leo Tolstoy " (Constable, London, 1905); " The Fruits of Enlightenment" (Luce, n.d.); " The Man Who Was Dead " (" The Living Corpse "), together with " The Cause of It All" (Dodd, Mead, 1912); "The Living Corpse" by Mrs. E. M. Evarts (Brown Bros., 1912); " The Light That Shines in Darkness " (Dodd, Mead, 1912). " The Nihilist " was " privately performed with much success," and " The Infected Family " never reached the stage; neither is published.

REFERENCES: Aylmer Maude, " Life of Leo Tolstoy " (Dodd, Mead, 1910); Aylmer Maude, introductions to " Plays by Leo Tolstoy " and " The Light That Shines in Darkness." For Tolstoy as a dramatist see Ashley Dukes, " Modern Dramatists." " A Literary History of Russia " by A. Brückner (London, Unwin, 1908) contains a chapter on mid-century Russian drama, and touches on Tolstoy as a writer of plays.*

* For a sketch on modern Russian literature see Grégoire Alexinsky, " La Russie Moderne" (Flammarion, Paris, 1912).

THE MAN WHO WAS DEAD

A play in five acts. Posthumously published 1912.
Translations published by Dodd, Mead, and Brown
Brothers.

" The Man Who Was Dead " is, like most of its
author's plays, written with a purpose: it is intended to show the evils of the Russian divorce
laws.   Besides being a thesis, or purpose play, it
is a character study; while Fedia is technically a
means to the author's ends, he is interesting as a
psychological study.

1. Although Tolstoy disregarded many of the
laws regulating the " well-made " play, he introduces certain of its elements, such as the conventional exposition and the delayed entrance of the
" hero."   The first departure from the trodden
path is the entire change of scene (Scene 2): the
playwright is by no means desirous of giving an
effect of unity to his first act.   But the play gains
in variety by this procedure, while a greater unity
is felt throughout, as a result of the fixing of our
attention upon the central figure: *he* is the unity
of the play.

2. The end of the first act is no less effective
than if it were carefully prepared; the way, for
example, a Pinero play is prepared.   The unemphatic " curtain " adds to the realism of the scene,
and the interest is carried forward, because the

audience has more, and knows it, to learn about
Fedia and his adventures. It might almost be said
that in this case the unemphatic ending becomes
emphatic.

3. Having determined that the theme of the
play was to be the divorce laws, and since one of
its chief points of interest was Fedia, the author
seems to have cared little how his work as drama
proceeded. The action is abrupt, and in places, a
little tedious. Observe, for instance, that
although in the second scene of the second act
Fedia declares that he will disappear in order that
his wife may be free to marry Victor, the resolution is not carried out nor the action developed,
until after the elapse of an entire act. The story,
per se, suffers.

4. After all the circumstances are made clear,
after the audience is familiar with the main characters, we may expect the " big scene." The last
act, laid in the Magistrate's office, is where Tolstoy
drives home his lesson, and makes his plea against
the laws. The scene is good, because it seems natural, the suspense is kept up and interest sustained
until the catastrophe, Fedia's suicide.

Court scenes and cross-examinations are nearly
always effective on the stage, as they are in life:*

* Emile Faguet, the eminent French critic, in his " Drame
ancien, drame moderne " (Colin, Paris), says: " Mankind
seeks in tragedy a pleasure which is born of the misfortunes
of mankind."

Galsworthy's " The Silver Box," and " Justice," Alexandre Bisson's " Madame X," Brieux's " Red Robe " and " Maternity " are good instances of this.

Note what Tolstoy does in this last scene: besides making his final plea against the law, he naturally ends his play with Fedia's suicide. What else does he do?

MAXIM GORKY

Maxim Gorky (Alexei Maximovitch Pyeshkov) was born at Nizhni-Novgorod, Russia, in 1868. Much of his youth was spent in such varied occupations as shoemaker's apprentice, surveyor, gardener, ship's cook, and baker. After obtaining a position as private secretary in his native city, he devoted himself largely to the writing of short stories and novels, depicting for the most part low-class types, peasants and tramps— his most successful characters.

The plays of Gorky are interesting chiefly because of the admirable qualities that go to the making of his fiction: realistic portraiture of the largest class in Russia, the serfs, and the low classes in the large cities. Gorky the dramatist in no way differs from his fellow dramatists as such; none of them has as yet acquired to any considerable extent the art of technique. Gorky, like other Russian novelists, is concerned rather with the delineation of human character and the questioning of life itself than with an artistic framework for his ideas.

PLAYS

The Lower Middle Class (1901).
The Lower Depths (Nachtasyl) (1902).
A few performances were given in 1902 in German at the Irving Place Theater, New York.

A Country House (1903).

Children of the Sun (1905).

Barbarians (1905).

Enemies (1906).

The Last (1908).   The Mother (1910).

Odd People (1910).   Children (1910).

"The Lower Middle Class" translated by Edwin Hopkins as "The Smug Citizen" (*Poet-Lore,* 1906); "A Night Shelter" by Edwin Hopkins (*Poet-Lore,* 1905), as "A Night Shelter," as "In the Depths" (*The Drama,* vol. xviii, Athenian Society, London), and as "The Lower Depths," by Laurence Irving (Duffield, 1912); "A Country House" as "Summer Folk" by Aline Delano (*Poet-Lore,* 1905); and "Children of the Sun" by A. T. Wolfe (*Poet-Lore,* 1906).

References: Ashley Dukes, "Modern Dramatists"; James Huneker, "Iconoclasts"; W. L. Courtney, "The Development of Maurice Maeterlinck" (Richards, London, 1904); Prince Kropotkin, "Ideas and Realities in Russian Literature."

THE LOWER DEPTHS *

A play in four acts. First published 1902. Translations as above.

"The Lower Depths" is rather a picture, or a series of pictures, than what we are accustomed to consider a play. It has no plot—that is, a developed story with a beginning, a middle, and an end,—it comprises a few more or less disjointed

* The play has been played in German in many countries under the title "Nachtasyl."

incidents.   The writer's purpose is merely to show
a number of characters, their motives and their
thoughts; he gives them certain situations as background, and not for any inherent interest that may
be in them.

1. Were a well-trained dramatist to treat the
material that goes to the making of this play, he
would doubtless have made the murder of Kostoloff a more important part of his story; would have
prepared, led up to and made much of it through
the preceding acts.   Yet the accidental nature of
the scene as Gorky wrote it is very realistic; the
suddenness is terrible, shocking.

2. The exposition in the first act is of very little
importance, for the past history of the characters
is told afterward by the people themselves; in fact,
the play is little more than a retailing of the lives
of the pitiful collection.   The " milieu," or environment, is felt at the rise of the curtain, without
the aid of spoken word.   The exposition, therefore, is of small importance, and the play starts
almost " at scratch."

3. Of development there is very little, for there
is hardly any plot to develop.   That section of the
play lying between the end of the exposition and
the climax consists mostly of talk, and may be considered as exposition of character.   For a moment
(p. 95, Irving translation) it seems that some sort
of plot were about to take root, but the incident is

not followed up, and is indeed not remembered until
the murder of Kostoloff, more than fifty pages
later.

4. The climax happens to fall where it belongs
in a conventionally constructed work: near the end
of the penultimate act. All technical canons are
merely the epitome of what has been found, by
natural evolution and continual experiment, to be
the best way of accomplishing an end; yet Gorky
has here, it seems, followed his natural artistic im-
pulses without reference to set rules. In passing,
be it remembered that rules are not arbitrary,
they are the summing up of the experience of those
who have learned and succeeded. In " The Lower
Depths " the climax is truly dramatic, exciting, as
Pepel strikes his victim; the scene is well handled
and, though abruptly, well developed up to the
very " curtain " of the act.

5. In the last act Gorky has only to show the
result of the murder and the influence of Luka.
We learn nothing of the first, but the second causes
a fitting and dramatic catastrophe. Luka has
left, and his influence is seen to be both beneficent
and evil. Satine quotes Luka in a speech that
contains the theme—so far as there is a theme—of
the play; " Why, [men] live for the better man,
dearie! Now let's say, there's carpenters and the
rest—masses—people. . . . And then out of them
a carpenter's born . . . a carpenter such as never

was in all the world: above 'em all: never was his
like for carpent'ring. 'E stamps 'imself on the
whole carpent'ring trade . . . shoves the whole
thing twenty years forward. . . . And so for all
the others. . . . Locksmiths then . . . boot-
makers and other working folk . . . and all the
agriculturals . . . and even the gentry—they live
for the better man! Each thinks 'e's livin' fer 'imself, yet it turns out it's fer that better man. A
'undred years . . . and maybe longer, we 'as to
go on livin' till the better man."—But, perhaps
ironically, the Actor "he's hanged himself!"
And the play ends with Satine's "Ah . . . he's
spoiled the song . . . the fool!"

6. Luka is the one bright spot in the play; technically, he serves as a contrasting figure to the
rest, while his prophetic optimism makes the hope-
less misery of his fellow-beings the blacker. He is
intensely Russian in his philosophic questioning
of the meaning and ultimate purpose of all life,
as well as in his inordinate desire to talk. Like
Turgenev's "Rudin," he is forever theorizing, and
that tendency is perhaps what has caused his
failure in life.

Compare the character of Luka with the Stranger in Jerome K. Jerome's "The Passing of the
Third Floor Back," Manson in Charles Rann Ken-
nedy's "The Servant in the House," and Gottwald
in Hauptmann's "Hannele."

TCHEKOFF

Anton Tchekoff * was born at Taganrog, Russia, in 1860. His early years were spent as assistant to his father, who was a provisions merchant. The youth was from the first a close observer of humanity, and continued to be so throughout his life. At the age of seventeen, he wrote a verse tragedy, which he afterward destroyed. Soon after, he entered the University of Moscow for the purpose of studying Medicine; at the same time he was engaged in the writing of short stories, the first of which was published in 1880. He then "secured a position connected with several of the smaller periodicals," and continued to print his stories, which were eminently successful. In 1880 he was graduated and, soon after, devoted himself to the practice of his profession. The year after the publication of his first collection of stories (1887) he was forced, on account of ill-health, to go south. Three years later he became resigned to a life of sickness. For almost the remainder of his years, he made his home in the Crimea, and there wrote five full-length plays, most of which were eventually successful. In 1904, the year of his death, when "The Cherry Orchard" was produced, Tchekoff came to be regarded

* Spelled variously Tchekov, Tchekhof, Chekhov, Chekov, etc.

as a dramatist of the first rank. He died in a little village of the Black Forest, in Germany.

As opposed to the more or less unconscious negligence of dramatic technique observed in the plays of Tolstoy and Gorky, we find in those of Tchekoff a deliberate intent to cast off most of the conventions clinging to established forms. This dramatist avoids the obvious struggles, the time-worn commonplaces and well-prepared climaxes that go to the making of most plays; he rather spreads out a canvas for our contemplation, not seeking to enlist our sympathies for individuals, but showing us merely the spectacle of humanity as he sees it. In so far as he succeeds in his attempt, his work becomes art, but because few audiences are able to lend their attention to apparently casual conversation and to the delineation of ordinary characters, his plays can be appreciated only by audiences which are sufficiently educated and interested in these things.

PLAYS

The Swan Song (1889).

A Proposal (1889).

Ivanov (1889).

A Boor (1890).

The Seagull (1896).

The Tragedian in Spite of Himself (1899).

The Three Sisters (1901).

Uncle Vanya (1902).

The Cherry Orchard (1904).

"The Cherry Orchard" is translated by Max S.

Mandell, and published as "The Cherry Garden" (under the supervision of the Dramatic Department of the *Yale Courant,* New Haven, 1908); under the title "Two Plays by Tchekoff," "The Seagull" and "The Cherry Orchard" are translated by George Calderon (Kennerley, 1912); "The Seagull" by Fred Eisemann (*Poet-Lore,* 1913); "Uncle Vanya," "The Seagull," "Ivanov," and "The Swan Song," by Marian Fell, as "Plays by Tchekoff" (Scribner, 1912); "A Bear" [A Boor], by R. T. House (Moods Publishing Co., New York, 1909); "A [Marriage] Proposal" by Hilmar Baukhage and B. H. Clark (French, 1915).

REFERENCES: Ashley Dukes, "Modern Dramatists" (Sergel, Chicago); Maurice Baring, "Landmarks in Russian Literature" (Macmillan, 1910); A. Brückner, "A Literary History of Russia" (Unwin, London, 1908); William Lyon Phelps, "Essays on Russian Novelists" (Macmillan, 1911); *The Drama,* vol. xviii (Athenian Society, London). The volumes containing translations by George Calderon, Max S. Mandell, and Marian Fell contain much additional material in their introductions; for a small bibliography, see *Bulletin of Bibliography,* October, 1912 (Boston Book Co.)—*Magazine articles: Quarterly Review,* vol. ccxvii (p. 27); *Bookman,* vol. xvi (p. 332); *Critic,* vol. xlv (p. 318); *Independent,* vol. lix (p. 299).

THE SEAGULL

A play in four acts. First published 1896. Translations by George Calderon and Marian Fell.

1. Keep well in mind that the dialogue in Tchekoff's plays is of the utmost importance. It has been well said that in this author's plays what is said is more important than what is done. Since this is so, we shall see that the dramatist does not bother to construct a plot which will interest or divert his audience.

The play opens with a conversation between Masha and Medvedenko; it is evident that a dramatic production is at hand. We also learn a good deal of the character of the two speakers. Soon after, another pair arrives, Sorin and Treplef. There is more talk, which is broken off by the entrance of further characters. The entire opening of the play is as casual as life itself. Nothing happens until (p. 34, Calderon translation) Nina appears in Treplef's play; but be it remembered, this play is merely an incident about which Tchekoff's own characters may converse.

Toward the end of the act Masha says to Dorn, ". . . Help me, or I shall commit some folly, I shall make havoc with my life. . . . I can't hold out any longer. . . . I am in pain. No one knows my sufferings. . . . I am in love with Constantine." Here is the thread of interest which is necessary—even in the plays of the radical Russian—to bridge the gap between the first and second acts.

2. In the middle of the second act, the plot is resumed—if the slender series of more or less connected incidents may be so termed—in the scene between Treplef and Nina, and further carried on in that between Trigorin and Nina. Interest is sustained and future events foreshadowed in Trigorin's words to Nina, regarding a subject for a possible story: " A girl—like yourself, say—lives from her childhood on the shores of a lake. She loves the lake like a seagull, and is happy and free like a seagull. But a man comes along by chance, and sees her and ruins her, like this seagull, just to amuse himself." This is a good example of foreshadowing. If the reader is at all familiar with the ways of dramatists, or of the authors of novels or short stories, he will at least suspect a definite application of such a speech and await the foreshadowed result.

For further examples of foreshadowing see those already mentioned in connection with the study of Ibsen's " Hedda Gabler," (p. 34 of this book) and the first act of Strindberg's " There Are Crimes and Crimes."

3. The third act contains a good deal of action, which is rather disjointed and " jerky "; the important part is the end, where Nina evidently

becomes Trigorin's mistress.—Notice that the scene was not prepared for, that it merely happened; that it occurred at the end of the penultimate act may be set down to the author's intent. He recognizes the value of climax, but in this case does not unduly emphasize it.

4. The last act contains the *dénouement;* this is, however, not all. There is further characterization. In this respect it differs from the usual last act, which is concerned mainly with the unraveling of the plot, and hardly at all with further characterization. The catastrophe is of course the death of Constantine.

5. Separate the plot proper from what is pure psychology. Has Tchekoff combined these two elements skilfully? Could he have created as interesting a play merely by using the plot and lightly sketching in the characters for the purpose of holding the plot together?

In considering this play,—and Russian plays in general—there arises the question of plot and character. How far can a dramatist interest his audience merely by presenting a number of people on the stage and analyzing them by making them tell their thoughts; or how far can he interest his hearers by placing puppets before us in more or less interesting situations? And how well can he combine the two processes? Much depends on the audience, much on the effect intended; the dramatist who aims only at the delineation of character for its own sake is bound to fail, as people do not and will not go to the theater for instruction alone. Nor can the dramatist who aims only at what is commonly termed amusement be worthy our consideration: a good dramatist is he who, while trying primarily to amuse, insinuates some philosophical truth, some interesting bit of psychology, some trait of human character into his play. One of the greatest of modern purveyors of amusement, the Frenchman Eugène Labiche, never wrote a play without some interesting comment on life, some whimsical turn of philosophical import—yet no one could accuse him of absolute frivolity, and certainly not of didacticism. As to Tchekoff, we feel that he has nearly succeeded in finding a medium for the expression of his thoughts and feelings, but that his plays fall short of perfection through their too great insistence upon character in the abstract.

ANDREYEFF

Leonid Andreyeff was born at Orel, Russia, in 1871. For a number of years he struggled to make a livelihood as a lawyer. He began writing about the year 1900, at which time he obtained a position on a newspaper. His first work was immediately successful, and attracted the attention of Gorky. The stories, a number of which have appeared from time to time in English and American periodicals, are mainly of a morbid and pessimistic turn, but their power and insight entitle them to a place among the best of modern fiction.

Those plays of Andreyeff which have been translated into English show a wider range of subject-matter and broader viewpoint than any Russian plays we have yet considered. Tolstoy deals with ordinary human beings, Gorky with those in the " lower depths," Tchekoff with middle and upper class " society," but Andreyeff, adopting a transcendental outlook, treats normal and abnormal people from a position of almost unearthly aloofness. In " Anathema " the characters are considered as mere puppets, the tools of higher and extra-terrestrial forces; in " To the Stars " they are placed on a high mountain—at the ends of the earth, one feels.

To say that Andreyeff is intensely Russian is little

more than may be said of Tolstoy, Gorky, or Tchekoff, but Andreyeff is if possible a truer representative
of his people than the others.   In him that disquieting
questioning of the end of life, that attempt to unveil
the meaning of the Universe, that pessimistic struggle
with overwhelming forces—are so strongly felt, that
nothing else is of much importance.   Here, it seems,
is the Slav incarnate.

PLAYS

To the Stars (1906).

The Life of Man (1906).

Ignis Sanat (or Savva)
    (1906).

King Hunger (1908).

Student Love (1908).

Night Love (1908).

Anathema (1909).

The Days of Our Life
    (1909).

Anfissa (1909).

Gaudeamus (1910).

The Black Masks (1910).

The Ocean (1911).

The Pretty Sabine
    Women (1911).

Honor (1911).

Love of One's Neigh-
    bor (1911).

Katerina Ivanovna
    (1912).

Professor Storitzyn
    (1912).

Thou Shalt Not Kill
    (1913).

An Event (1913).

The Parrot (1913).

The Thought (1914).

" To the Stars " is translated by Dr. A. Goudiss
(*Poet-Lore*, 1907); " King Hunger " by Eugene M.
Kayden (*Poet-Lore*, 1911); " Anathema " by Herman
Bernstein (Macmillan, 1910); and " The Pretty Sa-
bine Women " by Thomas Seltzer (*The Drama*, Feb.,
1914); " Love of One's Neighbor," translated by
Thomas Seltzer (*The Glebe*, January, 1914); " The
Life of Man," and " Savva," translated by Thomas
Seltzer (Kennerley, 1914).

REFERENCES: William Lyon Phelps, " Essays on Russian Novelists " (Macmillan, 1911). Introduction to Kennerley volume. *Magazines: Independent,* vol. lxvii (p. 242); *North American Review,* vol. cxciv (p. 882); *Living Age,* vol. cclviii (p. 786); *Lippincott's,* vol. xc (p. 241); and *The Drama* (Feb., 1914).

ANATHEMA

A tragedy in seven scenes. First published 1909. Translated by Herman Bernstein.

1. " Anathema " somewhat resembles Goethe's " Faust " in form and treatment; the Prologue, laid in " a wild deserted place, the slope of a mountain rising to infinite heights," at once strikes a note of vast and overwhelming immensity. The apprehension of the infinity of mysterious space pervades the air and becomes a half-felt background to the scene of human action.—Note how the setting as well as the high-sounding speeches of Anathema at once give the spirit of the Prologue.

This Prologue is a necessary division of the play, and is not merely a first act. Compare with it the Prologue to Goethe's " Faust " and that to Echegaray's " The Great Galeotto."

2. We have noticed how the opening scene of a play ought to tell what of the past must be known and what of the life and character of the participators in the story. But there is still another function to be fulfilled: the audience must understand the spirit of the play, they must be told

something of the manner in which the subject is to
be treated. In Björnson's "Leonarda," the
woman of that name exchanges a few words with
an old servant, at the very opening of the play,
and lets the audience know a little of the chief
character, in which it must interest itself for the
"two hours' traffic,"—and what the play is to be
concerned with. In "The Man Who Was Dead"
there is a similar scene. A play should "get into
the subject" before the audience loses interest.
Since "Anathema" is to treat of that questioning
of the ultimate purpose of life which we have seen
is characteristic of the Russian temperament, we
must early in the play be prepared for this. On
page 21, Sarah says, "Happiness! Who knows
what is happiness? All people are equal before
God, and yet one sells two cents' worth, while
another sells thirty cents' worth . . . and no one
knows why happiness is given to a person." Here,
in epitome, is the essence of the play; it is at least
an inkling of what it is to treat of.

8. It has been pointed out that the Russians
excel in portraying character, and we have seen
that Tchekoff's "Seagull" was written primarily
for the sake of the characters. It is pertinent
now to inquire into the nature of true characterization. What is it?

In this play, David is a striking example; he is
shown acting and speaking in accordance with

what the audience knows of him, in many moods
and under varying circumstances. The long
speech (pp. 52-53) in which he tells of the death
of his children and declares that he will not accept
the four million rubles, is a full revelation of what
we have been led to expect of such a man; just as
Sarah's washing Rosa's face is quite in accordance
with what we know of her. In succeeding acts,
David shows further traits as he is influenced by
other people and by force of circumstances, and
at the end he emerges a unified and logical character, fully portrayed—eminently human and
alive.

The great superiority of the Russians in this
field may be seen by comparing the chief personages of "The Man Who Was Dead," "The Lower
Depths," "The Seagull," and "Anathema," with
those, for instance, in many of the plays of the
modern French school. Brieux's "Three Daughters of M. Dupont" has some very good char-
acter-drawing, and Hervieu's "Know Thyself"
(Connais-toi) contains some memorable figures,
but the inferiority of the French to the Russian characters is undeniable. In the French
plays here referred to the theme is all-important,
and the characters are subservient—a means to an
end; with the Russians they are an end in themselves.

4. Andreyeff, like most of his race, writes with

little regard for accepted forms, yet with the true
instinct of the artist, for his play exemplifies the
" act unity " law. Each act contains a separate
and clearly defined incident, which stands out
above the other incidents, and advances the action
as well. The first act deals with the story of the
inheritance, the second, that of the renunciation.—
Notice how each of the last three acts contains a
unified story, and how each grows logically out of
the preceding.

It is highly interesting to note, in this study of
the Russians, how the accepted rules of dramatic
technique have been adhered to by some of the
most iconoclastic of playwrights; it is merely an
indication of the essential rightness of these laws,
it shows that rules of this sort are not arbitrary,
but are in the main the inevitable result of what
has been found right and proper and effective in
the past. The innovator should try to rid himself
of rules, but not until he knows what the rules are,
and how they have been applied in the past; in
many cases, he will find that essentially he has in
his apparently revolutionary attempt changed but
little.

AUGUST STRINDBERG

August Strindberg, Sweden's greatest dramatist, was born at Stockholm in 1849. At an early age he entered the University of Upsala, but was unable to support himself and continue his studies at the same time; in 1870, however, he returned to the University. He then began writing plays, and in 1872 an important drama, " Master Olof " was offered for production, but it was for six years continually refused by the managers. The play, when it finally appeared, is said to have inaugurated Sweden's dramatic renascence. Strindberg turned his hand to many things in these early years; he was schoolmaster, journalist, dramatist, writer of scientific and political treatises, and of short stories. In 1883 he left Sweden and traveled extensively in Denmark, Germany, France, and Italy, meantime publishing volumes of short stories, novels, and plays. The production of " The Father " in 1887 established his reputation as one of the most powerful dramatists of Europe. From that time on, his best plays, together with five autobiographical novels, followed. As a result of great intellectual strain and the painful proceedings incident to his divorce, Strindberg was forced to retire to a private sanitarium for over a year, but in 1897 he applied himself anew with added vigor to his work, and published a surprisingly large number of plays. He also established his Intimate Theater at Stockholm, where only his own plays were produced. In 1897, also, Strindberg returned to Sweden, where he remained until his death in 1912.—He was married three times; each marriage ended in divorce.

Strindberg, judged by the great majority of his works so far translated into English, is a dramatist endowed with a trenchant and searching power of analysis and remarkable insight into human nature; his chief plays are exact though narrow views of the feminine soul. His own experience was so unfortunate that his bitterness takes the form of a wholesale indictment of the sex. So far as he goes, it must be admitted that he is in the main just, but he fails to observe a proper balance. In " The Father," " Countess Julia," " Creditors," and " Comrades," he makes woman out a fiend incarnate. His greatest power lies in the portrayal of character, and the conflicts of human minds; he delights in showing the superiority of one individual over another. " The Father " is a good example, but " Creditors " is perhaps the finest mental duel, so to speak, in the range of modern drama.

PLAYS *

HERMIONE (1869).
THE OUTLAW (1871).
MASTER OLOF (1872).

* These "main works" are taken from Mr. Edwin Björkman's edition of the Plays of August Strindberg (Scribner, 1912).

THE SECRET OF THE GUILD (1880).

SIR BENGT'S LADY (1882).

THE WANDERINGS OF LUCKY-PER (1883).

THE FATHER (1887).

  Given in New York by Warner Oland 1912.

THE COMRADES (1888).

MISS JULIA (1888).

  Given in New York at matinées 1913.

CREDITORS (1890).   Little Theater, Chicago 1912.

PARIAH (1890).

  Given in New York at a matinée 1913.

SAMUM (1890).

THE STRONGER (1890).

  New York by the American Academy 1904.

THE KEYS OF HEAVEN (1892).

THE FIRST WARNING (1893).

DEBIT AND CREDIT (1893).

MOTHERLOVE (1893).

FACING DEATH (1893).

PLAYING WITH FIRE (1897).

THE LINK (1897).

TO DAMASCUS, I and II (1898).

THERE ARE CRIMES AND CRIMES (1899).

CHRISTMAS (1899).

GUSTAVAS VASA (1899).

ERIC XIV (1899).

THE SAGA OF THE FOLKUNGS (1899).

GUSTAVUS ADOLPHUS (1900).

THE DANCE OF DEATH, I and II (1901).

EASTER (1901).

MIDSUMMER (1901).

ENGELBRECKT (1901).
CHARLES XII (1901).
THE CROWN BRIDE (1902).
SWANWHITE (1902).
THE DREAM PLAY (1902).
GUSTAVUS III (1903).
QUEEN CHRISTINA (1903).
THE NIGHTINGALE OF WITTENBERG (1903).
TO DAMASCUS, III (1904).
STORM (1907).
THE BURNED LOT (1907).
THE SPOOK SONATA (1907).
THE PELICAN (1907).
THE SLIPPERS OF ABU CASEM (1908).
THE LAST KNIGHT (1908).
THE NATIONAL DIRECTOR (1909).
THE EARL OF BJÄLLBO (1909).
THE BLACK GLOVE (1909).
THE GREAT HIGHWAY (1909).

" The Father " is translated by N. Erichsen (Luce,
1907) and by Edith and Warner Oland (Luce, 1912);
" Miss Julia " as " Julie " by Arthur Swan (*Poet-
Lore*, 1911), as " Countess Julia " by Charles Recht
(Brown Bros., 1912), as " Countess Julie " by E.
and W. Oland (Luce, 1912), and as " Countess
Julia " by Edwin Björkman (Scribner, 1912);
" Creditors " as " The Creditor " by Mary Harned
(*Poet-Lore*, 1911); by Francis J. Ziegler (Brown
Bros., 1910); as " Creditors " by Edwin Björkman
(Scribner, 1912); " Comrades " by E. and W. Oland
(Luce, 1912); " There Are Crimes and Crimes " by

E. Björkman (Scribner, 1912); "The Dance of Death," I and II, by E. Björkman (Scribner, 1912); "Easter" by Velma Swanston Howard (Stewart and Kidd, Cincinnati, 1911), and by E. and W. Oland (Luce, 1912); "Swanwhite" by Francis J. Ziegler (Brown Bros., 1909); "The Dream Play" by E. Björkman (Scribner, 1912); "The Outlaw" by E. and W. Oland (Luce, 1912); "The Wanderings of Lucky-Per" as "Lucky Pehr" by Velma Swanston Howard (Stewart and Kidd, 1912); "Pariah" as "The Outcast" by Mary Harned [from the German] (*Poet-Lore*, 1906), as "Pariah" by E. and W. Oland (Luce, 1912), and by E. Björkman (Scribner, 1912); "Samum" as "Simoom" by Mary Harned [from the German] (*Poet-Lore*, 1906); "The Stronger" by F. J. Ziegler (*Poet-Lore*, 1906), by E. and W. Oland (Luce, 1912), and by E. Björkman (Scribner, 1912); "Debit and Credit" by Mary Harned [from the German] (*Poet-Lore*, 1906); "Motherlove" by F. J. Ziegler (Brown Bros., 1910); "Facing Death" by E. and W. Oland (Luce, 1912), and in *The Dramatist* (Easton, Penna., 1911); and "The Link" by E. Björkman (Scribner, 1912).

Scribners publish three volumes of Plays by August Strindberg, translated by Edwin Björkman; the first contains "The Dream Play," "The Link," and "The Dance of Death," I and II; the second, "Creditors," "There Are Crimes and Crimes," "Pariah," "Miss Julia," and "The Stronger"; the third, "Advent," "Simoom," "Swanwhite," "Debit and Cred-

it," " The Spook Sonata." The John W. Luce Co.
publishes two volumes also, translated by Edith and
Warner Oland, of which the first contains " The
Father," " Countess Julie," " The Outlaw," and " The
Stronger "; the second, " Comrades," " Facing Death,"
" Pariah," and " Easter."

REFERENCES: Huneker, " Iconoclasts "; Ashley
Dukes, " Modern Dramatists "; E. Björkman, " Voices
of To-morrow"; Archibald Henderson, " European
Dramatists " (Stewart and Kidd, 1914); among the
numerous introductions to the above-mentioned volumes of translations those in the Luce and Scribner
volumes will be found to be the fullest and most valuable. Among the numerous magazine articles, see
The Drama, No. 3, and *Bookman,* June, 1912.

THE FATHER

A play in three acts. First published 1887. Translated by (1) N. Erichsen, (2) Edith and Warner
Oland, and (3) Edwin Björkman.

1. " The Father " is a well constructed play ; it
contains one idea which is clearly stated, logically
and dramatically developed. The theme of the
play is, a woman's driving her husband to insanity
by making him doubt that he is the father of their
child. The dramatist goes to work immediately,
shows the man's ideas and habits, then the woman's,
and proceeds to show how she accomplishes her
purpose. He makes the husband a high-strung,
nervous man, and his wife a fiendish abnormal

woman; so that the dice are loaded to begin with. But, granted the characters, what they do is sufficiently natural to create the necessary illusion of reality.

The dialogue is economical and to the point; there are no long divagations, no unnecessary scenes of self-exposition—as in the plays of Tchekoff and Gorky;—conversation and action combine to reveal character.

As you read the play, notice how little is irrelevant, how each word adds to the totality of effect, the unity of the piece.

2. The purpose of the play is twofold: to paint the picture of Laura, and to tell the story as stated above. A few deft touches, and Laura is before us in flesh and blood. In the first act (pp. 25-6 of the Erichsen translation) the following dialogue takes place:

Laura

Then is it reasonable to think that one can see, by looking in a microscope, what is going on in another planet?

Doctor

Does he say he can do that?

Laura

Yes, he says so.

Doctor

In a microscope?

Laura

In a microscope, yes.

Doctor

This is serious, if it is so.

Laura

If it is so!   Then you have no belief in me, Doctor,
and I am sitting here and confiding the family secret
in you—

But when the Captain is questioned by the Doctor, it turns out that it was a spectroscope, not a
microscope, he had been using.   This is but one of
the many instances of how character is built up.
Find other examples of this in " The Father," and
see whether they advance the story at the same
time, or are merely incidental.

3. " The Father " is a psychological play; that
is, the action grows directly out of a mental struggle—in this case, it is a struggle or duel of the
sexes.   The climax therefore is reached when one
of the two contending minds, so to speak, dom-
inates the other.   This happens at the end of the
second act, where (p. 73) Laura tells her husband
that she has the means of putting him " under
control," in order that she may educate their
child " without listening to his advice "; she has
" his own letter to the doctor declaring himself to
be insane."   The Captain " looks at her in silence," while she tells him: " Now you have fulfilled

your function as an unfortunately necessary father and breadwinner. You are not needed any longer and you must go. You must go since you have realized that my intellect is as strong as my will, and since you will not stay and acknowledge it." Then "The Captain goes to the table, takes the lighted lamp and throws it at Laura, who escapes backwards through the door." She has conquered, by driving her husband to insanity.

The last act shows the result of Laura's " duel," and carries to a fitting conclusion her inhuman work.

4. You have doubtless noticed in reading the play that you are impressed by its appalling people and what they do; you are not touched or led to pity any of the characters, unless it be the little daughter. The father, though he ought to be an object of compassion, is so brutal, so uncompromising—whatever the reason—that we can have little sympathy for him. We feel more horror than pity, and that is because Strindberg has made his characters almost incarnations of their bad qualities; they are for the most part abnormal and neurasthenic, and as such do not appeal to us as average, healthy beings would. There is a certain relief when the Captain is taken away; we are sure he will be better off away from his wife— indeed, it is rather disappointing that Laura is not sent to a sanitarium. Had Strindberg drawn here

a more sympathetic victim, his play would have
been much more effective, more terrible, and less
purely horrible.

5. An interesting parallel is suggested in
Laura's quoted lines at the end of the second act,
to one of the principal ideas in Bernard Shaw's
" Man and Superman." What does Shaw's Tan-
ner owe to Strindberg's Laura?

THERE ARE CRIMES AND CRIMES

A comedy in four acts.   Originally published 1899.
Translated by Edwin Björkman.

This " comedy " belongs to a later period in
the mental development of Strindberg. In " The
Father," the tone is one of fierce denunciation, in
" There Are Crimes and Crimes " there is little
recrimination, but rather a Slavonic questioning
of existence, and a firmer hold on life; the author
has conceived higher ethical standards. In his
own words,* " Light after darkness; new produc-
tivity, with recovered Faith, Hope, and Love—
and with full, rock-firm Certitude." In this frame
of mind, he set to work on a play which should
teach, or rather expose, the working-out of a
higher code of morals than that which passes current in our ordinary court-room. The play shows

* Quoted in Edwin Björkman's introduction to " There
Are Crimes and Crimes " (Scribner, 1912).

that the greatest crimes are the spiritual crimes done against oneself, one's higher nature, and that the law has nothing to do with them.

1. Given so abstract a theme as the struggles of a conscience, what is the best way to write a play illustrating it? To allow the personages in a play to talk about and around a theme, is obviously only a makeshift, for in that case the drama is not the true medium of expression for the author. In a play we demand action, it is the prime requisite. In this play, however, the author shows in terms of actuality the result of a mental attitude, and not merely talks about it or permits his characters to do so. Maurice says (p. 24), ". . . if we had to answer for our thoughts, who could then clear himself?" and, as if to test this statement, Strindberg places Maurice in a position where his thoughts really do result in acts, and shows how he succeeds in clearing himself. That is the play.

2. By dividing each act into two scenes, the author creates a greater feeling of verisimilitude. There is a rhythm, an ebb and flow, in life which is often lacking in even good plays, but which is felt in this, largely by reason of the division of acts into two scenes each.

On a smaller scale, this rhythmic quality is well defined in the quarrel scene at the end of the third act of Henry Arthur Jones's " Dolly Reforming

Herself." There the action mounts and falls, giving a consummately skilful reproduction of the
pulsation of life.

3. It has been pointed out that practically
every important event in a play should be prepared for in advance, and in most cases worked up
to. When (p. 49) the Abbé announces to Adolphe
and Mme. Catherine that Marion is dead, the news
is a shock to the audience. Is there any reason
for this apparent violation of the above-stated
law? Why should this news shock? Why should
the audience not be given some hint?

Find similar examples of such surprises in other
modern plays.

4. The difference between this kind of play and
the average American or English production of
to-day may be observed by comparing the scene
(pp. 49-52) where the Abbé and the Commissaire
announce that the Parisian public are up in arms
against Maurice for what they believe to be the
murder of his daughter, Marion. The Commissaire speaks for a whole page, and the Abbé adds
to the story from time to time. This is really a
modernization of the Greek method whereby a messenger tells the story of the disaster which has
happened off-stage. The American dramatist
would make a more vivid and appealing scene, by
concretely showing the wrath of the public. Edward Sheldon does this in the " big act " of " The

Boss," where the townspeople are just outside the house of the principal character of the play, throwing stones through the window and breaking the furniture in the room. This expedient is by no means confined to the American and English drama, for Ibsen's " An Enemy of the People " and Hauptmann's "Weavers" contain similar scenes; but the point to be made here is that such procedure is common with dramatists writing for English-speaking audiences.

5. Strindberg is a master of his art. When he violates the laws of stagecraft and goes counter to the fundamentals of technique—or seems to do so —we may be sure that he has sufficient reason. The third act in a four-act play is one which is vitally important. Few dramatists, having successfully conducted their story up to this point, can neglect it and introduce a long dialogue having little to do with the plot. The third act of this play opens with such a dialogue, which is interrupted only with the news of Marion's death. This is an important incident no doubt, yet it is the only one which breaks a long and discursive scene. This continues until the entrance of Henriette, eight pages later, and from then on until the end of the scene, which is in itself effective.

What reasons can you offer for this treatment of this particular scene?

HAUPTMANN

Gerhart Hauptmann, acknowledged the foremost
living German dramatist, was born at Obersalzbrunn,
Silesia, November 15, 1862. His early schooling he
received in his native town and in Breslau; this was
followed by work on his uncle's farm. But Hauptmann preferred to study sculpture, and went to the
art school in Breslau, then Jena, and finally to Italy.
In 1885 he married, and made Berlin his home until
1891, when he returned to Silesia—after embarking in
a new dramatic venture inaugurated in 1889, the German Free Theater—having by that time begun to win
recognition as one of the leaders of the new Naturalistic school. His first play, " Before Dawn," was
produced at the Free Theater in 1889, and was considered the first important example of the new movement in Germany. Besides numerous plays, Hauptmann has written poems, and a few novels and stories.

Hauptmann is undoubtedly one of the finest poets
of modern times, and his choice of the field of drama
is by some critics regretted. He is far from successful as a dramatist, and still seems uncertain as to
which kind of play form best suits him. Owing to
this hesitancy he has often failed, owing first to the
unsuitability of his medium, and second to his lack of
experience. Hauptmann is ever experimenting with
form; it would be difficult to name any more than two

or three of his plays which are built on a noticeably
similar plan and are akin either in structure or subject
matter. " The Weavers " is most unusual, for it
is concerned with a whole community, rather than
a few " important " characters, and there seems to be
little relation between the acts. " The Sunken Bell,"
on the other hand, centers around one man; while
" Michael Kramer " is an almost equally divided study
of two men. There are likewise poetic tragedies, and
comedies, and folk dramas and middle-class tragedies.
It is doubtful whether Hauptmann will ever find
exactly the best form into which to mold his thoughts.
Still, by his exquisite poetry, his delicately attuned
temperament for the reception of every impression,
and his incontestable dramatic genius, he is easily
one of the greatest of living dramatists.

PLAYS

BEFORE DAWN (1889). New York, in German, first
produced Irving Place Theater.

THE FESTIVAL OF PEACE (1890). In an adaptation
by Donald Robertson, Chicago 1907.

LONELY LIVES (1891). New York in German 1898;
matinées in English 1902.

THE WEAVERS (1892). New York in German 1895;
in English by the Hull House Players, Chicago
1911.

COLLEAGUE CRAMPTON (1892). New York in German 1895.

THE BEAVER COAT (1893). New York in German
1910.

HANNELE (1893).

New York in German 1893-4, in English 1894, and in 1910 by Mrs. Fiske on tour.

FLORIAN GEYER (1896).

THE SUNKEN BELL (1897).

New York in German by Frau Sorma 1897, in English by Sothern and Harned 1899 on tour.

DRAYMAN HENSCHEL (1898).

New York in German 1912.

SCHLUCK AND JAU (1899).

MICHAEL KRAMER (1900).

THE RED COCK (1901).

POOR HEINRICH (1902).

ROSE BERND (1903).

ELGA (1905).

AND PIPPA DANCES (1906).

THE MAIDENS OF THE MOUNT (1907).

CHARLEMAGNE'S HOSTAGE (1908).

GRISELDA (1909).

THE RATS (1911).

GABRIEL SCHILLING'S FLIGHT (1912). New York in German 1912.

THE FESTIVAL PLAY (1913).

THE BOW OF ODYSSEUS (1914).

All German productions in New York were at the Irving Place Theater, which has produced much of the best contemporary German drama.

"Before Dawn" is translated by Leonard Bloomfield (*Poet-Lore*, 1909), and by Ludwig Lewisohn (Huebsch, New York, 1912); "The Festival of Peace" by Roy Temple House, as "The Reconciliation" (*Poet-Lore*, 1910), and by Janet Achurch and

C. E. Wheeler, as the "Coming of Peace" (Sergel, n.d.); "Lonely Lives" by Mary Morison (Heinemann, London, 1898); "The Weavers" by Mary Morison (Huebsch, 1911); "The Beaver Coat" by Ludwig Lewisohn (Huebsch, 1912); "Hannele" by William Archer (Heinemann, 1898), by Charles Henry Meltzer (Doubleday, Page, 1908), and by G. S. Bryan (*Poet-Lore,* 1909); "The Sunken Bell" by Charles Henry Meltzer (Russell, New York, 1902, later Doubleday), and by Mary Harned (*Poet-Lore,* 1898); "Fuhrmann Henschel" by Marian A. Redlich (Sergel, 1910), as "Drayman Henschel" by Ludwig Lewisohn (Huebsch, 1913); "The Red Cock" as "The Conflagration" by Ludwig Lewisohn (Huebsch, 1912); "Rose Bernd" by Ludwig Lewisohn (Huebsch, 1913); "Elga" by Mary Harned (*Poet-Lore,* 1906); "And Pippa Dances" by Mary Harned (*Poet-Lore,* 1907); "The Rats" by Ludwig Lewisohn (Huebsch, 1913). B. W. Huebsch has so far published two volumes of a collected "Dramatic Works" of Hauptmann, which is to contain all the plays. The first volume contains "Before Dawn," "The Weavers," "The Beaver Coat," and "The Conflagration"; the second, "Drayman Henschel," "Rose Bernd," and "The Rats." About the time this book appears a third volume containing "The Reconciliation," "Lonely Lives," "Colleague Crampton," and "Michael Kramer," and a fourth including "Hannele," "The Sunken Bell," and "Henry of Aue," are promised.

REFERENCES: Huneker, "Iconoclasts"; Dukes,

" Modern Dramatists "; E. E. Hale, Jr., "Dramatists
of To-day"; Otto Heller, "Studies in Modern German
Literature " (Ginn, Boston, 1905); Alfred Stoeckius,
"Naturalism in the Recent German Drama," with
special reference to Hauptmann (Columbia University, 1903); Georg Witkowski, "German Drama of
the Nineteenth Century" (Holt, 1910); Kuno Francke,
" Glimpses of German Culture " (Dodd, Mead, 1898)
for " Florian Geyer " and " The Sunken Bell ": introduction to the Huebsch edition.—*Magazines: Poet-
Lore,* vol. xxii, No. 2; *The Critic,* vol. xxxiv (p. 225);
Contemporary Review, vol. lxxxix (p. 370); *Edinburgh Review,* vol. cciv (p. 447); *Atlantic Monthly,*
vol. lxxxi (p. 71); *Arena,* vol. xxxiii (p. 251); *Living
Age,* vol. ccxxxiv (p. 156); *Fortnightly,* vol. lxxvi (p.
459); and *Quarterly,* vol. cxci (p. 317); " The Bulletin of Bibliography " (Boston Book Co., 1911) contains a bibliography of Hauptmann.

THE WEAVERS

A play in four acts. First published 1892. Translated by Mary Morison.

As one of Hauptmann's experiments in dramatic form, " The Weavers " is highly significant.
Instead of a hero, he has created a mob; this mob
is therefore the protagonist—or chief character;—and if individuals emerge from the rank and
file they are not thrust into the foreground to stay
long.   It is the weavers as a class that are ever
before us, and the unity of the play is in them and

in them alone; they are only parts of a larger picture which will take shape as the story advances, and are not intended to be taken as important individuals.

1. Hauptmann may be said to have created a new form of drama in " The Weavers," and that form is what may be designated as the tableau series form, with no hero but a community. As the play is not a close-knit entity, the first act is casual, and might open at almost any point; and since it starts with a picture, or part of a picture, there is hardly anything to be known of the past. The result is that no exposition is needed. The audience sees a state of affairs, it does not lend its attention and interest to a story or the beginning of a plot or intrigue. This first act merely establishes the relation between the weavers and the manufacturers.

There is no direct hint given in the first act as to what is to come in the second; the first is a play in itself, a situation which does not necessarily have to be developed. It does, however, prepare for the revolt, by showing the discontent among the downtrodden people, and it also enlists the sympathy of the audience.

2. Act two is another picture, this time that of the homes of the weavers; the effect produced is one of blackest misery and unrelieved poverty. Two points should be noticed: first, the dramatist

develops some characters, like Mother Baumert and Ansorge, but only to a certain extent, for fear of their overshadowing the chief business of the play, which is the presentation in concrete form of the oppression and struggles of the weavers; and second, the plot—such as it is—is started by Jaeger. But this plot is not permitted to absorb the interest of the audience, it is rather brought in almost as an incident, and does not attain to great proportions until a large number of the weavers participate, later on. And when that happens, the plot and characters have an equal claim upon our attention.

This act does look forward; it throws out tentacles of interest, for when Ansorge says, "We'll stand it no longer! We'll stand it no longer! Come what may," the audience knows that trouble is ahead, and wants to see its result.

8. The third act carries the plot forward, and gives a further picture of the life of the weavers, this time a little less sordid than in the foregoing acts. The change of scene is made primarily in order to give variety to the whole picture, and also to furnish a likely gathering place for the instigators of the rebellion. The end of the act brings the plot to a higher degree of development, and increases the suspense; Hornig's words, " It'll not surprise me if this ends badly," are clearly prophetic, and prepare for the next act.

4. Between the third and fourth acts the rebellion has come to a head, and the weavers start on their warpath of depredation. The contrast in setting is again good; this time we are in the luxuriously furnished home of the capitalist. Soon we are aware of the presence of the wild crowd outside, and know that the revolt is making quick headway. The entrance of Jaeger as a prisoner, his subsequent release by the mob, the evacuation of the house by its owners, the entrance of the weavers, the despoiling of the rich furnishings, all supply excellent dramatic action. By the end of the act, the weavers are like wild animals, whom nothing can curb. Here, then, is the culmination of the action: the climax.

What more is expected? Clearly, the result of what has happened. Will the weavers conquer?

5. The last act must terminate the rebellion, but the mere ending, in the defeat of the strikers, is not sufficient to fill an entire act; there must be something further. Hauptmann has therefore introduced an incident that will supply the need. The "reactionary" weaver is accidentally shot. The purpose of this is doubtless to drive home the irony of fate, in this case the uselessness of revolt. This bit of action is very skilfully interwoven, and leaves us with a keen appreciation of the wrongs of the weavers, by reason of its vividness—also because it is the last incident of the play. While

it is true that we sympathize with the weavers as
a class up to the last act, we lack the personal element. For example, we may read in a newspaper
that five thousand people die of the famine, but
until we see the mother dying in an effort to feed
her child, or the father killing his family outright
rather than see them starve—until we see these
things individually—they will not touch us.

HANNELE

A dream-poem in two parts. Originally published
1893. Translations by William Archer, Charles
Henry Meltzer, and G. S. Bryan.

" Hannele " is described by the author as a
" dream-poem." With that description in mind,
as well as the text which is prefixed to the beginning of the printed edition—" Suffer the little
children to come unto Me, and forbid them not.
For of such is the Kingdom of Heaven "—there
should be no difficulty in adopting, as it were, a
sympathetic method of attack.

1. The play deals with the " assumption " of
Hannele Mattern; everything is subsidiary therefore to the character of and circumstances concerning the child. This centralizing process,
whereby the interest is directed to and fixed upon
a single figure, is the exact contrary to that employed in " The Weavers," where an entire community is the " hero."

Whereas in "The Weavers" no character was developed to the detriment of the others and to the picture as a whole, in "Hannele" there is nothing—no incident or character—which does not contribute to the delineation and eventual development of the little girl.

2. The division into two acts is unusual; the first is concerned with one part of Hannele's illness, the last with her "assumption." The so-called "acts," or parts, have no well-defined unity, but serve the purpose of balancing and dividing the action.

Using your knowledge of the principles of act division as applied to the plays already considered, put "Hannele" into three acts, then four, then five. What is the most satisfactory of these arrangements?

3. The patent purpose of the sordid scene with which the play opens is to provide variety; by this means contrast between the squalor of the alms-house and the purity and innocence of the child's vision is the more striking. This contrast is most effective when Hannele first appears upon the scene, Gottwald protecting her; while Hanke, Hete, and Seidel quarrel among themselves. And at the end of the play there is a contrast, a bold relief to the sordidness of Hannele's entire existence: the triumph of the poetic, the highest ideal of the purity of childhood, summed up in the Stranger's Song.

4. William Archer * calls attention to the fact that " Hannele " has no " conflicting wills," and yet is a "moving drama." † The English critic undertakes to disprove the theory formulated by the French critic, Brunetière,‡ that "the theater in general is nothing but the place for the development of the human will, attacking the obstacles opposed to it by destiny, fortune, or circumstances." Archer admits that this struggle of human wills against obstacles is *one* of the essentials of drama, but that it is not a necessary factor. In support of his statement, he cites " As You Like It," " Ghosts," and " Hannele," in which the struggle, if there is one, is of but minor importance. Of what, then, does the "moving" quality in this play consist ? It is the result of the keenly sensitive touch which is felt to be the spirit of the work, one of sweetness created by the character of Hannele, and the triumph of her soul over her sordid environment. It is therefore the poet and the psychologist in Hauptmann, and not primarily the dramatic artist, that have risen above rules and regulations, so that in this play at least Brunetière's statement is hardly less capable of application in spite of the apparent contradiction.

* "Playmaking," chap. iii: " Dramatic and Undramatic."
† See Introduction, present volume.
‡ "Etudes Critiques," vol. vii, pp. 153 and 207; quoted in Archer.

The above discussion leads naturally to the
question whether those qualities in Hauptmann,
which have stood him in such stead in default of
technical skill, could not have been used to better
advantage in a story or a poem or a novel, where
they would not have to be subjected to the ever-
changing interpretations of the actor and the
more or less brutal realism of the mechanics of the
stage.* This is the crux of the matter: Has
Hauptmann chosen the right medium? Is " Hannele " a play at all?

THE SUNKEN BELL

A play in four acts. First published 1897. Translated by Charles Henry Meltzer.

" The Sunken Bell " is without doubt Hauptmann's best known play. It is not, however, his
most representative piece of work: Hauptmann is
so many-sided that three plays at least must be
read in order to obtain some definite idea of his
total output.

1. The question of influences,† nearly always
a very precarious one to discuss, constantly arises

* Mrs. Fiske's production of " Hannele," a few seasons
ago, was one of rare insight and beauty, so that the argument does not in this case apply.

† It is interesting to note in this connection that two
English critics recently drew parallels between Galsworthy's
" Silver Box " and Hauptmann's " Weavers," and spoke of
the indebtedness of the English dramatist to the German.

in connection with the plays of the author under consideration, and it is at least safe to assert that " Before Dawn " shows distinct traces of Tolstoy, " Lonely Lives " and the " Sunken Bell " of Ibsen. Even Goethe has been suggested as a probable source of Hauptmann's inspiration in the last-mentioned play. Maurice Huret has well said that " Henrik Ibsen was at once a naturalist and a symbolist. . . . This combination, though apparently contradictory, is effected in perfect harmony, which is the result of the labor of supreme genius. Hauptmann was incapable of so great an effort." * Instead of welding into a harmonic whole the diverse elements of realism and poetry in " The Sunken Bell "—as Ibsen did in " Peer Gynt "—he has had recourse to a more primitive procedure: he places side by side scenes of everyday realism and scenes of faëry romance; much as Shakspere did in the " Midsummer Night's Dream." Whether Hauptmann purposely adopted this method or whether he was unable to attain the white heat necessary for that complete welding, is not easy to determine, nor very much worth while discussing.

In a letter to a London paper Galsworthy replied that he had never read a line of Hauptmann, and that he had merely heard that " The Weavers " had something to do with a strike.

* In " La Littérature allemande d'Aujourd'hui " (Perrin, Paris, 1909).

2. The eternal question of What is a play? again arises in connection with " The Sunken Bell." Certain critics of the first rank declare that this play is good poetry but poor drama, others that it is good drama, as well as good poetry. It has been pointed out in the Introduction to the present Outline * that the standards are changing so rapidly nowadays that there is no criterion whereby to judge of the technical validity of a play. Mr. Clayton Hamilton † states that " A play is a story devised to be presented by actors on a stage before an audience." The same critic also declares (speaking of Browning's " Pippa Passes " and " The Sunken Bell ") that " These poems are not plays; and the innocent spectator, being told that they are, is made to believe that poetic drama must be necessarily a soporific thing." And yet, " The Sunken Bell " is " a story devised to be presented by actors on a stage before an audience." We must conclude, then, that although it is a play, it is not a *good* play; or else that the definition above quoted is not sufficiently inclusive. " The Sunken Bell " is not a good play in the sense that Sardou's " Divorçons " is a good play—a *pièce bien faite:* —it lacks unity, the story is not well developed, it wants swiftness of action, and clarity. Nor is it a good play in the sense that Bernard Shaw's

* See p. 6 ff.
† In " The Theory of the Theatre," p. 3.

" Man and Superman "—a work which is not a
" well-made play "—is good. Hauptmann's play is
good because of a combination of qualities—some
of which may indeed be unnecessary—psychological interest, some dramatic poetry, as distinguished from purely lyrical, a fairly well-constructed plot, and the bodying forth of the truth
in concrete form that the artist must ally himself
with and understand Nature if he is to realize what
is best in himself.

3. " The Sunken Bell " is, among other things,
a study in temperament, the so-called " artistic
temperament." In this play, the poet is chiefly
interested in the psychological development of the
artist, Heinrich. We are told that he is a great
artist, but the fact is not made clear to us. A
German critic * takes Hauptmann to task because
Heinrich does nothing to prove that he is what he
is claimed to be. He aptly remarks that the
more and the better Heinrich speaks the less are
we inclined to believe in him, for most true artists express themselves best through the medium of
their chosen art. In the drama we must believe
what we are told. A dramatist of necessity asks
his audience to take certain things for granted—
such as the lapse of time and the resultant foreshortening of events,—and the audience, having

* Prof. E. Sulger-Gebing, in " Gerhart Hauptmann "
(Teubner, 1909).

accepted these premises, is ready to give credence to what follows. In " The Sunken Bell," we must firmly believe that Heinrich is a true artist— otherwise the author has failed. This is a question which the student must answer for himself.

Among the numerous studies in temperament, compare those in D'Annunzio's " Gioconda," Bataille's " La Femme nue," * Hauptmann's " Michael Kramer," Georges de Porto-Riche's " La Chance de Françoise," and Hermann Bahr's " Das Konzert." † How do these authors make their artists " live "? ‡

DRAYMAN HENSCHEL

A play in five acts. Originally published 1898. Translations by Marian A. Redlich and Ludwig Lewisohn.

" Drayman Henschel " has little in common with the two preceding plays; it is not a picture of a community, nor is it poetic in form or supernatural in treatment. It is a realistic " folk " or " bourgeois " tragedy, a psychological study of

* Not translated. It was produced in England under the title of " Dame Nature."

† Not translated. Produced in an American adaptation— as " The Concert "—by David Belasco.

‡ Further studies in temperament may be found in Tchekoff's " The Seagull," Sudermann's " Magda," and Brieux's " Ménages d'Artistes." The Brieux play has not been translated.

the moral degeneration of a woman. Hanna is the
central figure, the unity of the play. Henschel is
merely the victim.

1. Hauptmann shows a series of steps in the
demoralization of his chief character; the audience
in this case may *see* her develop. Ibsen's method,
in his later plays at least, is almost the reverse.
He would doubtless have begun * this play at the
fourth act, summed up the substance of the first
three in a short exposition, and expanded the last
two. This is what he did in the " Doll's House,"
" Ghosts," and " Rosmersholm." Much may be
said in favor of both these methods, but in this
particular case Hauptmann's gives the greater
illusion of life, as we can believe what we actually
see unfolding before our eyes more readily than
we can what is told us at second-hand.

2. Hauptmann's method in this play demands
a broader canvas, with more incidents and a
greater number of characters than would the swift-
moving and compact method of Ibsen. Hauptmann has therefore introduced a number of super-
numeraries into his story which serve no purpose
but to create atmosphere and throw sidelights on
Hanna's character and to a lesser extent aid the
plot. In " Rosmersholm " each person forms an
integral part of the story, and each at the end of

* See Clayton Hamilton's article, " Where to Begin a
Play," *Bookman*, January, 1913.

the play is satisfactorily disposed of; in "Dray-man Henschel" the greater part are forgotten, merely subsiding, and gradually or abruptly pass-ing into oblivion. Ibsen ties the loose threads, Hauptmann leaves them hanging in the air, Ibsen gives an illusion of greater compact unity, Haupt-mann that of life itself, where the loose threads are rarely gathered up, much less tied together.

This statement applies only to the present play, for in "The Weavers" all the characters are lost in the picture; there is no satisfactory end to that play, properly speaking; in like manner, Ibsen introduces casual characters to advance the story of "Brand" and "Peer Gynt."

Find further instances of the application of these principles; such instances are easily found in the plays of Björnson and Strindberg.

3. The fifth act is in itself perhaps the most interesting in the play, especially as regards the mental evolution of Henschel. With great skill his character is developed from the beginning to the end of the act. An atmosphere of terror, a feeling of suspense, a haunting fear of impending tragedy, unite to make the scene an unforgettable one.

Suicide as an expedient for closing a play has often been discussed, and its justification the sub-ject of a great deal of debate. If a dramatist gets his hero or heroine into trouble and is embarrassed

as to how to rid himself of them, suicide is the
shortest way out of the dilemma.   The suicides in
" Hedda Gabler," " The Man Who Was Dead,"
" The Lower Depths," " The Seagull "—to mention only those plays which have so far been
studied—are all natural results, not simple ex-
pedients for the purpose of ending the plays ; in
each case the event is prepared for and worked
up to.   But the question arises, does not an over-
constant use of this method—whether it be justified or not—tend to lessen its horror?   Galsworthy's " Justice " and Masefield's " The Tragedy of Nan " end each with a suicide, but in both
cases the suicides seem inevitable : any other solution would be false to life and to art.   Still, the
question remains.   These instances are surely justified.   But what of the suicides that end Clyde
Fitch's " The Climbers," and Pinero's " The Second Mrs. Tanqueray "?

SUDERMANN

Hermann Sudermann was born September 30, 1857, at Matziken, in East Prussia, Germany. After attending school at Elbing and Tilsit he became at the age of fourteen a druggist's apprentice. His university training was received at Königsberg and Berlin. Soon after his graduation from college, he entered the field of journalism, and from that into literary work of a higher order. His first important works were novels, several of which—" Dame Care," " Regina," and " The Song of Songs "—are well known to English readers. In 1889 he produced his first play, " Die Ehre " (Honor), which met with great success.

Sudermann is essentially a man of the theater, a dramatist by instinct; he has little of the poetic beauty and deep insight into human character which constitute the chief charm of Hauptmann's work, but he has at his command all the tricks of the trade, a perfected technique, that make him on the whole a greater dramatist than his celebrated contemporary. Of these two recognized leaders of the modern German stage, Hauptmann is the poet and idealist, Sudermann—although not devoid of ideals and not at times without a certain beauty—is the craftsman.

PLAYS

HONOR (1889).

New York frequently in German, in English matinée 1905.

THE DESTRUCTION OF SODOM (1891).

New York in German 1892-3.

HOME (Magda) (1893).

New York in German 1894, in English at various times by Mmes. Modjeska, Patrick Campbell, Fiske, and others.

THE BATTLE OF THE BUTTERFLIES (1895).

New York in German 1907-8.

HAPPINESS IN A NOOK (1896).

New York in German 1896.

MORITURI: Teja, Fritzchen, and The Eternal Masculine (1897). "Fritzchen" was given in New York in German 1902; in English by the Yale Dramatic Association 1914.

JOHN THE BAPTIST (1898).

New York in German 1901, in English by Sothern and Marlowe 1906-7.

THE THREE HERON'S FEATHERS (1899).

ST. JOHN'S FIRES (1900).

New York in German 1901, Boston in English, January, 1904, by Nance O'Neil.

THE JOY OF LIVING (1902).

New York in German 1903-4, in English by Mrs. Campbell 1902 and on tour.

STORM-BROTHER SOCRATES (1903).

AMONG THE STONES (1905).

THE FLOWER BOAT (1905).

New York in German 1906-7.

ROSES: Streaks of Light, Margot, The Last Visit, and
The Faraway Princess (1907).

CHILDREN OF THE STRAND (1910).

THE BEGGAR OF SYRACUSE (1911).

A GOOD REPUTATION (1912).

New York in German October, 1913.

THE HYMNS OF CLAUDIAN (1914).

" Honor " is translated by Hilmar Baukhage (Samuel French, 1914). "Home" is translated as
" Magda " by C. E. A. Winslow (Samuel French,
1911); " Morituri " (three one-act plays, " Teja,"
" Fritzchen," and " The Eternal Masculine "), by
Archibald Alexander (Scribner, 1910); " Morituri,"
" Teja " (the first of the above-mentioned one-act
plays), by Mary Harned (*Poet-Lore,* 1897); " John
the Baptist " by Beatrice Marshall (Lane, 1908),
and as " Johannes " by Mary Harned (*Poet-Lore,*
1899); " The Three Heron's Feathers " by H.
T. Porter (*Poet-Lore,* 1900); " The Fires of St.
John," " translated and adapted by Charles Swick-
ard " (Luce, 1904), by Charlotte Porter and H. C.
Porter (*Poet-Lore,* 1904), and by G. E. Polk (Wil-
son, Minneapolis, 1905); " The Joy of Living " by
Edith Wharton (Scribner, 1903); " Roses " (four
one-act plays, " Streaks of Light," " Margot," " The
Last Visit," and " The Faraway Princess "), by
Grace Frank (Scribner, 1909).

REFERENCES: E. E. Hale, Jr., " Dramatists of To-
day "; Ashley Dukes, " Modern Dramatists "; Otto
Heller, " Studies in Modern German Literature "

(Ginn, 1905). For "John the Baptist" see Kuno Francke's "Glimpses of Modern German Culture" (Dodd, Mead, 1898).—*Magazines: Poet-Lore,* Summer, 1911; *Atlantic,* vol. lxxxi (p. 71); *Westminster Review,* vol. cliv (p. 553); *Living Age,* vol. ccxxxiv (p. 156); *Critic,* vol. xvii (p. 61); *International Review,* vol. vi (p. 140); *Outlook,* vol. lxvii (p. 74); and *Forum,* vol. xxvi (p. 374).

HONOR

A play in four acts. Originally published 1888.
Translated by Hilmar Baukhage.

"Honor" is of considerable historical importance: the first play of its author, it was among the first to be produced at the new German Free Theater (Freie Bühne) in 1889, and, together with Hauptmann's "Before Dawn" (1889), ushered in the new dramatic movement of "Youngest Germany."

The Naturalist movement in literature, in which Tolstoy, Zola, Ibsen, and Strindberg were the leaders, bore fruit in France with the Théâtre Libre, founded by André Antoine in 1887, and in the German theater above mentioned. The new movement aimed at two things: the delineation of character in as truthful a manner as possible, and the presentation of problems and theses directly affecting the society of the day. These ideas were by no means new, but the combination of greater adherence to external details—usually "unpleasant" and often brutally shocking—and "purposefulness" was decidedly novel.

1. As nearly every literary work is the result of influences, it is pertinent to inquire into Sudermann's first dramatic experiment. Emile Augier, together with Alexandre Dumas fils, were the originators of the modern " social " play: " The Son of Giboyer," " Madame Caverlet," and " The House of Fourchambault " are pictures of middle-class life as well as social documents, each carrying with it a definite thesis or " moral." The " Demi-Monde," " Claude's Wife," and " Madame Aubray's Ideas," of Dumas fils, were written primarily to prove a thesis, preach a social sermon.

Sudermann's " Honor," therefore, is not original in treatment or idea, but the fact that his play was written and produced in Germany in the late eighties was of national importance. The German drama at that time was at nearly its lowest ebb, and the infusion of new blood was greeted with more friendly criticism than the inherent value of the play merited.

Honor was the subject of his story. Ibsen once said, " If, in placing upon the stage certain persons whom I have known or seen, certain facts of which I have been a witness or which have been related to me, and, in throwing an atmosphere of poetry over it all, I happen to awaken a soul within them, various ideas will take root in the minds of the different characters: that is the point of departure. I cannot help it if in my own brain, as I write, various ideas come to me. That is merely accessory; the first principle of a play is action, life." (From a conversation quoted by Prozor, the French translator of Ibsen.)

Is Sudermann more interested in the thesis than in the play as a dramatic entertainment? Did he write " Honor " as a stage piece, or did he write it in order to promulgate his ideas on honor? The text will reveal his intentions.

2. Is " Honor " a thesis play in the sense that " Magda " is? Which is the better art, and why? Compare the two plays.

3. Trast is the " Raisonneur " of the piece. He exposes the author's ideas. How does he do this? Does he accomplish the author's ends skilfully, or not? In his words and acts, does he gently insinuate the conception of honor which Sudermann wished the audience to get, or does he deal out in long speeches sections, as it were, of a tract? Compare the " Raisonneurs " in " The Great Galeotto," "Magda," and "There Are Crimes and Crimes," with Trast. To how great an extent may a dramatist legitimately project himself and his ideas through the agency of a " Raisonneur "?

4. It has often been observed that the plays of the last few years tend to do away with the " big scene " at the end of the act. How has Sudermann managed his " curtains "?

MAGDA

A play in four acts.   Originally published 1893.
Translated by C. E. A. Winslow.

Magda is one of the finest technical accomplish-
ments in all modern drama; practically every element of the well-made play—unity, clearness, and
a well-defined struggle—is here skilfully adapted
to a modern theme.

1. The entire first act is exposition, exposition
of the best kind.   The important characters are
introduced, or—as in the case of Magda herself—
so constantly spoken of that they are well known
before they appear; the history of the past is
unfolded, the spirit of the " home " makes itself
felt almost immediately, and the struggle between
the old and the new, between Schwartze and Magda, set in movement.

Note that the play actually starts, the wheels
are set going, the moment Schwartze (p. 45) tells
Heffterdingt, " Then God's will be done."

2. While the opening act sets the scene, as it
were, for the subsequent action, the second is concerned with Magda's homecoming and her reception; also her resolution to stay with her family.
But, in the scene between her and Heffterdingt,
more past history is revealed; it will be used later
in the play.   This is preparation.   Yet one thing
further is accomplished by this scene: the stipula-

tion that Magda shall not be questioned as to her
past life. The family agree to this, and all goes
well—up to the very last page of the act, where
Heffterdingt ("Struck by a new thought") says,
". . . Yes, I am sure she will confess everything
herself." This line is sufficient to arouse the sus-
picions of a careful auditor or reader.—Will she
confess? And if she does, what will be the result?

3. The contrast between the old and new orders,
—between the old German idea of home and the
new idea of individual development, begun in the
first act,—is continued throughout the play; in the
first act, the spirit of the old was brought before
us by means of conversation, in the second, it is set
forth in the struggle between two persons—
Schwartze and Magda—and in the third it is both
discussed and "acted." Magda's playful banter,
the little humorous touches in her scene with the
servants, the provincial wonderment of Franziska
and Mrs. Schwartze, all contribute to the central
idea. In addition, the first few pages of the third
act form an interlude between the rising action of
the second and the tension that is to increase later
in the third act. The scene between Magda and
Marie (pp. 91-95) is a "bridging section" or
connecting link between the "interlude" and the
Heffterdingt-Magda and the Schwartze-Magda
colloquies, which are followed by further scenes of
varying tension, through that between Magda and

Von Keller, to the culminating point in the act, in which Schwartze and his " erring " daughter go into the former's room, each having " something to say " to the other.

4. So far, the end of each act has been emotionally higher than the beginning, as well as tenser than the end of the preceding. The first, second, and third acts have each culminated in a crisis; while the end of the third act was the greatest crisis—that fraught with the utmost importance to the chief characters—in the play: that was the beginning of the climax. But the actual climax occurs off-stage in the interval between the third and fourth acts. This is a more effective method than as if the clash had occurred upon the stage, because we see the beginning, imagine the struggle, are ignorant for a few moments of its outcome, and when the curtain rises on the last act, are still in suspense. In this way, there is no relaxation of pressure. The climax started in one act, is carried over into the next and does not end until Schwartze enters (p. 130), as we see, defeated.*

* Another good example of this is in William C. De Mille's play, " The Woman." A cross-examination is begun at the end of the second act, the curtain falls, and when it rises on the last act, the examination is still in progress, but is nearly at an end. The culminating point, however, is not reached until a little later in the act. Here, then, the climax, begun at the end of the penultimate act, does not end until well on into the last.

From that point on, the action subsides quickly
to the catastrophe, where (p. 155) it rises momentarily, then falls to the " curtain."

FRITZCHEN

A drama in one act (in " Morituri "). Originally
published 1897. Translated by Archibald Alexander.

The one-act play * is concerned with a single
incident as a rule, and aims at " totality of effect "; its exposition is briefer, and its action usually swifter than in plays of more than one act.

1. Like certain others of Sudermann's plays—
" Honor " and, to a lesser extent, " Magda "—
" Fritzchen " deals with the question of honor.
It is tragedy of ironic circumstances. The utter
futility of the sacrifice of a promising young man
to the conventions of the German code of honor is
driven home with great power and vividness.
Observe that there is no struggle, no opposing
wills: only a situation from which there is no escape. Fritz is the victim of his father's training
and of the " laws " of honor to which he is subject.

2. " Fritzchen " is one of the best examples of
the one-act play, because of its unity, its swiftness,
and its power to create a single, dominant, lasting
impression.

* See *Bookman,* April, 1913.

A comparison of this play with Bernard Shaw's
" Press Cuttings " (1909), called a " topical
sketch," shows the superiority of the German over
the English—or Irish—play. Shaw crowds half
a dozen incidents into his sketch, Sudermann but
one; Shaw's work lacks unity, Sudermann's gives
its very essence.

The one-act play, a condensed form, should
suggest, just as the longer play develops. The
one-act play is too short to allow of very
much development, either of story or character:
it must present without comment what it sets out
to present, and take the auditor at once to the
heart of the subject. In a longer play the dramatist has time to prepare the scene for the action
that is to come; in the shorter he must sketch the
scene in a few words or by means of a deft bit of
" business," and proceed at once to work. In the
preface to his one-act plays in the volume entitled
" Embers " (1911), Mr. George Middleton speaks
of his plays as being " studies in consequences and
readjustments, being, in fact, a further expression
of some preceding situation. Each play is, therefore, the epitome of a larger drama, which is suggested in the background."

WEDEKIND

Frank Wedekind was born in Hanover, 1864. He was forced to study law, though his natural inclination was for writing, which he found time at an early age to do. In Zurich, where he later continued his studies, he came into contact with some of the "Moderns," among them Hauptmann and Strindberg. In 1888, after the death of his father, Wedekind went to Munich, and thence visited London, Paris, and "all the centers of European culture, all the sinks of its perversity and crookedness. He squandered his money and his beliefs recklessly. In 1891 he returned again to Munich." * A few years later he was imprisoned for *lèse majesté*, was soon released and became a vaudeville performer, then acted in his own plays, and eventually settled in Munich, after his marriage in 1906.

Wedekind is of no school, he recognizes no established laws, he sets at defiance morality and accepted belief; some of his plays contain scenes that "would sicken a police reporter," while the most innocuous often contain scenes that are sickeningly brutal. Yet withal, he is a genius—if by that term we mean one who has the art of presenting life and character, of

* Maximilian Harden, quoted by Pollard, "Masks and Minstrels."

creating illusion, one capable of producing a thing of power and beauty. If this is granted, then Wedekind is an exceptional genius. His unparalleled audacity, his reckless iconoclasm, his absolute disregard for accepted forms in art, cannot fail to command respect.

PLAYS

THE TENOR (1900).

THE MARQUIS OF KEITH (1901).

SUCH IS LIFE (1902).

PANDORA'S BOX (1904).

THE AWAKENING OF SPRING (1905).
  Produced, German Theater, New York, 1912, for
    two or three performances.

THE DANCE OF DEATH (1906).

THE LOVE POTION (1907).

THE YOUNG WORLD (1907).

THE EARTH SPIRIT (1907).

MUSIC (1908).

OAHA (1908).

CENSORSHIP (1908).

HIDALLA (1908).

THE PHILOSOPHER'S STONE (1909).

FRANZISKA (1912).

CASTLE WETTERSTEIN (1913).

SAMSON (1914).

  "The Tenor," as "The Heart of a Tenor," is adapted by André Tridon (*The Smart Set*, June, 1913); "Such is Life" is translated by Francis J. Ziegler (Brown Bros., 1912); "The Awakening of Spring" by the same (Brown Bros., 1910); "The Earth Spirit" by Samuel A. Eliot, jr. (Boni, New York).

REFERENCES: Ashley Dukes, "Modern Dramatists"; Percival Pollard, " Masks and Minstrels of New Germany."—*Magazines: Current Literature,* vol. xlv (p. 204). See also the introduction to the English version of the " Awakening of Spring."

SUCH IS LIFE

A play in five acts. First published 1902. English version by Francis J. Ziegler.

1. This play is written with no distinct unity of action; yet the character of the King forms a nucleus that gives a certain unified impression to the work. Wedekind has no regard for developing the play as a story or a framework for characterization, he merely strings together a series of scenes and says what he wants to say; when he is through he rings down the curtain.

Yet, compared with the " Awakening of Spring," " Such is Life," is conventional in treatment. The former is a series of disjointed conversations, some brutally naturalistic, some homiletic, and others supernatural. There is little selection of material, no arrangement with a view to dramatic effectiveness, and no emotional modulation. In the latter play there is at least coherence, for it relates in almost chronological order— and in chronicle form—the fortunes of the dethroned King.

2. The play is a cynical laugh at Man. One of

the characters in the "Awakening of Spring"
says "the living are not worth compassion"; their
petty ambitions, Wedekind seems to say, their sys-
tems of caste, their ideals even, are worth but a
laugh.   Here is the King, he is reduced to beg-
gary, and has finally become jester at his own
court.   When he declares that he is the King and
starts to adduce the proofs—"too late, too late—
Such is life!"—he dies.

A comparison of Wedekind's play with Strindberg's "Dream Play" and "Lucky Pehr" will
bring out some interesting points.   What is the
essential difference between Wedekind and Strindberg in their treatment of somewhat similar
themes?   Structurally, and as to the idea or philosophy set forth in them?

SCHNITZLER

Arthur Schnitzler was born at Vienna in 1862. He was graduated from the University in that city in 1885, and has ever since devoted himself to the practice of Medicine, together with the writing of novels, short stories, and plays.

Schnitzler's plays are the epitome of the highly cultivated and rather superficial life of the aristocratic classes of present-day Vienna. They treat, with grace and charm, of the young well-bred lover and his mistress, in an ever-changing succession. In some of the more characteristic plays—like " Anatol " and " Roundels "—the subject is the breaking-off point of the relation between the two, and in others the tragic, or rather the pathetic side is seen—as in " The Legacy " and " Light-o'-Love. With his quiet cynicism and reminiscent moodiness, he is " content to take as his theme only a few scenes from life, and even in those few scenes he recurs continually to a single passage." His philosophy of life might well be expressed in one of his own lines, " We all play parts, happy he who knows it."

PLAYS

The Fairy Tale (1895).
Anatol (1895).

Five episodes from "Anatol," produced, Little
Theater, New York, 1913.

Light-o'-Love (1896).

Produced, German Theater, New York, 1896; in
English as "The Reckoning" 1907.

Free Game (1897).

The Legacy (1899). American Academy 1912.

The Green Cockatoo
Paracelsus } three one-act plays.
The Companion (1899)

"The Green Cockatoo," produced, New York, in
German 1907-8; in English by Mrs. Fiske on
tour 1910.

The Veil of Beatrice (1900).

Living Hours
The Woman with the Dagger
Literature } four one-act plays.
The Last Masks

Produced in New York in German 1907-8.

Roundels (1903).

The Lonely Way (1904).

Intermezzo (1905).

The Call of Life (1906).

Puppet Plays: The Puppet Player, Brave Cassian,
The Great Puppet Show (1906).

Countess Mizzi (1909). Stage Society, N. Y. 1913.

Young Medardus (1910).

The Distant Land (1911).

Professor Bernhardi (1912).

Produced in New York in German 1914.

"Anatol" is paraphrased by Granville Barker
(Kennerley, 1911); "Light-o'-Love" is translated

by Bayard Quincy Morgan (*The Drama,* August, 1912); "The Legacy" by Mary L. Stephenson (*Poet-Lore,* 1911); "The Green Cockatoo, Paracelsus, and The Companion," in one volume, by Horace B. Samuel (Gay and Hancock, London, 1913), the "Green Cockatoo" as "The Duke and the Actress" by Hans Weysz (*Poet-Lore,* 1910); "Living Hours" by Helen Tracy Porter (*Poet-Lore,* 1906); "The Lady with the Dagger" by Helen Tracy Porter (*Poet-Lore,* 1904). "The Green Cockatoo," "The Mate," and "Paracelsus," translated in one volume, are announced by McClurg; "The Lonely Way," "Intermezzo," and "Countess Mizzi," translated with introduction by Edwin Björkman in one volume (Kennerley).

REFERENCES: Percival Pollard, "Masks and Minstrels of New Germany" (Luce, 1911); Ashley Dukes, "Modern Dramatists." See introduction to the Gay and Hancock volume.—*Magazines: Poet-Lore,* vol. xxiii, No. 1; *The Drama,* August, 1912; *Fortnightly Review,* vol. xciii (p. 447); *North American Review,* vol. cxcvi (p. 635); and *Current Literature,* vol. li (p. 670).

LIGHT-O'-LOVE

A play in three acts. First published 1896. Translated by Bayard Quincy Morgan.

1. Schnitzler is usually at his best in the one-act play, but in "Light-o'-Love" he has combined the qualities that are characteristic of the shorter

pieces with a sense of structure unusual in his more ambitious efforts. This play is quite simple in form and contains few points that need detain us. —If you compare the light and graceful treatment of the same theme in the " Anatol " " sequence," with the no less graceful but pitiful treatment in the present play, you will see Schnitzler's methods well exemplified. In "Anatol" the man is the central figure; for him the continual change is picturesque, perhaps lingeringly sad, but never tragic; in "Light-o'-Love" the man takes the affair too seriously, and is killed, while the heroine goes off, presumably to kill herself.

2. Quick and witty dialogue is one of the greatest assets in this play—as in practically all of the same author's—and it is fortunate that " Anatol " and " Light-o'-Love " are so well translated as to give a re-creation to a considerable extent of the spirit and " esprit " of the original.

Dialogue is a very important element in the drama, and its cultivation a rare quality. * The best dialogue reveals character, and advances the plot, creates atmosphere, and is interesting and

* It is not, however, imperative. Many of the most effective scenes in modern drama—in Galsworthy's "Justice," for instance, and Max Reinhardt's production of "Sumurûn," are carried on partly or entirely without the use of words.

attractive in itself. At the same time, it should
not be so brilliant as to detract from the play, or
so long or involved as to become uninteresting.
Such plays as Oscar Wilde's "Lady Windermere's Fan" or "A Woman of No Importance"
undoubtedly suffer from their superlatively brilliant array of wit, while Donnay's "Return from
Jerusalem" is far too detailed and expository
throughout to interest an average American audience; though a French one, better accustomed to
listen to plays with involved dialogue, will listen
with rapt attention. The first act of "Light-o'-
Love" is a model of good dialogue. From the entrance of Christine (p. 20) to the end of the act,
the conversation seems as easy and natural as in
life. In reality it is not; it is a very compressed
and carefully selected arrangement of seemingly
natural speeches, each containing a point that advances the story, reveals character, or else is a necessary connecting link between such speeches.

Henry Bataille (in *Les Annales*, Paris, No.
1536), himself a master of the art of dialogue,
speaks of "Style in the Drama": "The so-called
style of the theater is true to life neither in appearance nor in actuality; it is neither conversation nor the language of the emotions. . . . It
is a sort of written language, with a syntax such
as that employed in the novel, . . . it is the
natural outcome, pure and simple, of the situation

or the characters.   These expose everything, even
their ideas, to the public.   This is the essence of
convention. . . . The art of dialogue is a
moulding of the observation of nature; that must
ever be kept in view."

VON HOFMANNSTHAL

Hugo Von Hofmannsthal, who, together with Schnitzler and Bahr, represents the Viennese school of drama,
was born in Vienna in 1874. His first work, a dramatic poem, was written when he was but seventeen
years of age. Two years later his play "Death and
the Fool" attracted considerable notice from the
critics. Since these early years he has produced
plays steadily, and has risen in the estimation of his
countrymen to the front rank of poets.

The setting to music of his "Electra" and "Rose-
Cavalier" by Richard Strauss (they were first given
as operas in New York in 1910 and 1913) has added
much to his fame.

Percival Pollard says of Von Hofmannsthal: "His
is a triumph of Viennese verbal confectionery applied
upon material as old as the centuries. His is the
absolute final point to be reached in mere beauty,
mere literary skill. He has added nothing to the
Sophocles stories he modernized, save artifice. When
he tried to be dramatic without aid of his enchanting
versification, in his prose play 'Christina's Heim-
reise', 1910, he failed completely; that episode proved,
had it been necessary, that as a dramatist he has never
had proper inspiration, however lovely he has been as
a poet."

PLAYS

YESTERDAY (1891).

THE DEATH OF TITIAN (1892).

DEATH AND THE FOOL (1893).

THE EMPEROR AND THE WITCH (1895).

THE MINE IN FALUN (1897).

THE WOMAN IN THE WINDOW (1899).

THE WEDDING OF SOBEIDE (1902).

THE ADVENTURER AND THE SINGER (1902).

ELECTRA (1904). New York, Mrs. Campbell 1907-8.

VENICE PRESERVED (1905—Translated from Otway).

ŒDIPUS AND THE SPHINX (1906).

ŒDIPUS REX (Translated from Sophocles) (1910).

CHRISTINA'S HOMECOMING (1910).

THE ROSE-CAVALIER (1910).

ARIADNE AT NAXOS (1912).

Arthur Symons has translated "Electra" (Brentano, 1908). "Death and the Fool" is translated by Elizabeth Walter (Badger).

REFERENCES: Ashley Dukes, "Modern Dramatists"; Percival Pollard, "Masks and Minstrels of New Germany" (Luce, 1911).

ELECTRA

A tragedy in one act. First published 1904. Translated by Arthur Symons.

1. The poet has chosen to put his ideas into an ancient mould, and the result is not a little bewildering. Does he intend to present in "Elec-

tra " merely a Greek play, or does he wish to use
the Greek form as a frame through which to observe modern character?   These questions raise a
doubt as to the advisability of pouring new wine
into old bottles, for it cannot be denied that this
play loses most of what was Greek in Sophocles,
and that the modern thought and characterization
of Von Hofmannsthal suffer from the alien form
into which they have been forced.   If the Austrian
poet wished to produce merely a translation of
Sophocles, he has of course failed ; and if he wished
to give a characterization of an abnormal modern
woman—which he has done—he has chosen the
wrong medium, or at any rate, the least effective.
There is, however, one further consideration, the
poetry of the original German.   This, in spite of
the admirable translation, it is quite impossible to
reproduce, but as style is after all of secondary
importance in drama, it is not imperative to take
it into account, in judging the play as a play, so
that we can make a just estimate on the strength
of our English version.

2. The poet has made of Electra an intensely modern and abnormally over-wrought woman ; he has substituted for the spiritual motive
of revenge (in the Greek play) a personal and
almost pathological hatred.   This shifting of motives takes most of what is Greek out of the play.
But, granting that the modern dramatist has not

selected the best form in which to present his ideas or sing his poetry, how well has he accomplished the task which he has set himself?

The play is above all effective; morbid, perhaps, even melodramatic—but undeniably effective theatrically. And it is unified: Electra is kept before us continually, and the story revolves about her. The literary style, as we have said, we are unable to judge in this version, but we are assured that it is " unsurpassed " as to " sheer diction, sheer lyric form."

BECQUE

Henry Becque, the acknowledged originator of the modern French Naturalistic school, was born at Paris in 1837. His early works were produced in the 'sixties, but " La Parisienne " and " The Crows," his most important plays, were peddled about for years before they obtained a hearing. During the last years of his life, Becque was recognized as the master, the founder of one of the most important movements of modern times. He died in 1899.

The production of " The Crows " (Les Corbeaux) in 1882 at the Comédie Française and " The Parisian Woman " (La Parisienne) at the Renaissance in 1885 marked the beginning of the new school which, in 1887, under the leadership of André Antoine, had a theater of its own, the famous Théâtre Libre, or Free Theater. It was Antoine's idea to give an opportunity to original dramatists of producing, without fear of the censor and without dependence upon the likes of the public, naturalistic plays, as well as to introduce, more or less as models, the plays of Tolstoy, Ibsen, Strindberg, and Björnson.*

Becque is a Naturalist because his characters are

* For further discussion of the Théâtre Libre, see Augustin Filon, " Modern French Drama " (Chapman and Hall, London), George Moore, " Impressions and Opinions " (Brentano), and Barrett H. Clark, " Four Plays of the Free Theater " (Stewart & Kidd, 1915).

living beings, because they give the illusion of reality, and because his technique is subordinate to and of less importance than his characterization. He writes because he wishes to give us a " slice of life "; he has no lesson to teach, no sermon to pronounce, no thesis to prove. His plays, in the words of a French critic, " are life " itself. Huneker says, " Becque's major quality is his gift of lifelike characterization. Character with him is of prime importance. He did not tear down the structure of the drama, but merely removed much of the scaffolding which time had allowed to disfigure its façade."

PLAYS

MICHEL PAUPER (1871).

THE MERRY-GO-ROUND (1878).

HONEST WOMEN (1880).

THE CROWS (The Vultures) (1882). American Academy 1905.

THE PARISIAN WOMAN (1885).

THE BUFFOONS (unfinished) (1912).

In the " Théâtre Complet " (Paris, 1899), the following miscellaneous pieces are included: " Sardanapalus," " The Prodigal Son," " The Elopement," " The Virtuous Women," " The Start," " Madeleine," " Widowed," " An Execution," and " A Four-handed Game."

" The Crows " is translated by Bénédict Papot (*The Drama,* No. 5, 1912), " The Vultures," " The Woman of Paris," and " The Merry-go-round," by Freeman Tilden (Kennerley).

REFERENCES: Huneker, "Iconoclasts"; Ashley
Dukes, "Modern Dramatists"; Augustin Filon,
"Modern French Drama" (Chapman and Hall, London, 1898, out of print). *The Drama,* No. 5, 1912,
and the introduction to the Kennerley volume.

THE CROWS

A play in four acts. First published 1882. Translations by Bénédict Papot and Freeman Tilden.

1. The first act is mainly exposition, and this
is, with its long speeches, asides, and soliloquies,
what we should term to-day very old-fashioned. A
glance over the first acts of Pinero's "The Thunderbolt" or Galsworthy's "The Pigeon" will show
the great progress in mere technique that has been
accomplished within the past three decades. Yet
in this particular play Becque is not concerned
with the finer touches incident to the handling of
his plot, his interest is centered in the characters,
and admirable pictures he paints in this first
rather clumsy act! Vigneron's opinions on music,
and his wife's kindly patronage of Merckens—she
knows "he is only an artist, but doesn't want to
make him feel his inferiority"—are touches that
"place" the bourgeois and his wife at a single
stroke.

The death of Vigneron, announced just as the
curtain falls on the first act, is a little unprepared
for, but the author wished it to shock his audience.

This is also merely exposition, in that it is preparation for the important business of the play, which
has not yet begun; the play does not properly
begin until the beginning of the second act. As a
matter of fact, the whole first act could be put into
a page or two of exposition and placed at the
beginning of what is now the second. But Becque,
knowing what he was about, wished to prepare the
" milieu " with all possible care, and there is little
question that the method he adopted was the best.

2. There is one striking difference in the manner of treatment between this play and what is
most representative of the Frence drama of to-day.
Such playwrights as Lavedan, Donnay, and Capus, are " finished " writers, as to style and construction; Becque is brutal and direct, unpolished,
and since the people he for the most part por-
trays are not in " society," they are frequently
more life-like than if they were.*

The transition from scene to scene is abrupt,
especially in the first act, too abrupt to give the
illusion even of that rhythm of life which is so
great an asset in all representations of life. Read
pages 49 and 50; there are parts of three distinct
episodes, and yet there are no modulation, no
blending, no " bridging sections." More skilled,

* These remarks hold true largely of " The Crows." " The
Woman of Paris " (La Parisienne) is carefully written, in
places delicate, but never brutal.

though perhaps less inspired dramatists, would have welded these incidents, blended them into a harmonious section of transition: Donnay has done this with signal success in most of his plays, in " La Douloureuse " repeatedly.

3. The second act is typical of Becque; although it shows the influence of Molière, it has a savage note of satire, and a brusque and peremptory movement all its own. The three " crows " scene is one of the most bitterly ironical in the realm of modern drama.—After reading this act, one is led to believe that no other than the uncouth and unrhythmical treatment employed by Becque could be better adapted to the subject-matter. The act is that of a cynical Molière.

4. It is in the third act that we find a good deal of this sort of material that was developed later by Hervieu and Brieux. Becque throws out a suggestion—the injustice of the law and its abuse —and Hervieu later develops it in " The Nippers " (Les Tenailles); or he shows the impossibility of an unmarried woman's making an honest living, and Brieux writes " Blanchette " and " The Independent Woman " (La Femme Seule). This is what the critics mean when they speak of " The Crows " as being the Bible of the modern Naturalists.

5. The play has what is known as an unemphatic ending. Conventional plays of the school

of Scribe and Sardou end with what in America is called a " punch,"—a " big " scene. This is effective, but the other method is no less so, merely because of its very unobtrusiveness. Often, the unemphatic ending contains a sting, a satirical touch that sums up the act, or, in some instances, the theme of the entire play. Galsworthy's "Strife" is a case in question; Tench says to Harness, " D'you know, sir—these terms, they're the *very same* we drew up together, you and I, and put to both sides before the fight began? All this —all this—and—what for?" and Harness answers, " That's where the fun comes in!" and the curtain drops. In Louis N. Parker's pseudo-historical comedy "Disraeli," the first act is another example of the unemphatic ending. This is quite a common practice nowadays, and the reason for it is chiefly that it heightens the illusion. In life, the exciting is mingled with the commonplace, and one of the most interesting and dramatic things in life is the strange contrast between the sublime and the commonplace, between the tragic and the comic. Therefore, in place of ending his act or his play with a scene of great tension or high emotion, the dramatist seeks to reproduce parts of life, makes a still more lifelike and exciting scene, and places one of these contrasted moments at one of the most critical points of his act or play: the last. Perhaps one of the bitterest end-

ings of any play is that to Wedekind's "Music."
"At the end, when Klara, after undergoing im-
prisonment, exile, poverty, public disgrace and the
loss of her beloved child, finds herself bereft of
even Reissner's regard, she is led away in a stupor
from the miserable attic. It is then, in reply to
a wish of the physician that she will suffer no
lasting mental disturbance, that Lindekuh pre-
ludes the fall of the curtain by the caustic remark: 'She'll be able to sing a song.' " *

The emphatic last act will be considered in connection with another play, Echegaray's "Madman or Saint." (See p. 219 of the present
volume).

* From Francis J. Ziegler's preface to his translation of
Wedekind's "The Awakening of Spring."

LEMAITRE

Jules Lemaître was born in 1853 and received his early education in a small town in Touraine. Later he completed his preliminary and higher studies in the capital, and taught literature in Le Havre, then in Algiers, and still later in Besançon and Grenoble. At the age of thirty-one he came to Paris to live permanently, where he was offered the position of dramatic critic on the *Journal des Débats*. At that time he was known as the author of a slight volume of delicate verses—" Les Médaillons "—and a few finely-written and clearly conceived criticisms. These were the first of a collection which have since appeared in seven volumes as " Les Contemporains." The dramatic criticisms were collected, in ten volumes, as " Les Impressions de théâtre." Lemaître's first venture into the realm of the drama was with " Révoltée " (The Woman Who Revolted) in 1889; although this play was not very successful, the author wrote a number of social comedies of the first order, the best of which are " The Pardon " (1895), and " La Massière " (The Studio Assistant, 1905). Lemaître is likewise the author of a number of short stories and one novel. Lemaître died early in August, 1914.

PLAYS

THE WOMAN WHO REVOLTED (1889).

DEPUTY LEVEAU (1890).

A BLANK MARRIAGE (1891).

FLIPOTE (1893).

THE KINGS (1893).

THE DIFFICULT AGE (1895).

THE PARDON (1895).

GOOD HELEN (1896).

THE ELDEST DAUGHTER (1898).

THE STUDIO ASSISTANT (1905). New York, as " Poor
    Little Thing," 1914.

THE PRINCESSE DE CLEVES (not produced).

BERTRADE (1908).

THE MARRIAGE OF TELEMACHUS (with Maurice Don-
    nay) (1910).

" The Pardon " is translated by Barrett H. Clark,
" Three Modern Plays from the French," (Holt,
1914).

REFERENCES: " Modern Plays from the French "
(Holt, 1914).

THE PARDON

A comedy in three acts. First published 1895.
Translated by Barrett H. Clark.

Technically the most interesting feature of this
comedy is the fact that it has only three characters.
The sheer interest of the material, the dialogue, and
the acting must make up for the lack of variety. The

dramatist's methods can be more easily observed in this play than in almost any other.

1. The French dramatist—the European dramatist, in general—has this advantage over the American: he knows that his audience will listen to dialogue, and be interested in the psychological study of character. This does not, however, mean that he can do without action and variety, only that his auditors are more used than the Americans to listening to the more or less leisurely and detailed analysis of human motives. It is probable that no American audience would be prepared to listen to " The Pardon " on the stage, not because it lacks interest, but because it lacks, or appears by comparison with most plays to lack, movement. Lemaître wishes to tell us of the mental processes of Georges, Suzanne, and Thérèse under certain circumstances. That is " The Pardon."

If an American had taken this theme and these characters and wished to write a " successful " play, how would he have gone about his work?

2. The " Ménage à trois," or the household composed of husband, wife, and lover, has for many years been a favorite subject with French writers, both of novels and plays. They have often, chiefly by foreigners, been criticised for this over-insistence on the eternal " triangle." Is the criti-

cism valid? Taking the " Ménages à trois " in
" The Labyrinth," the skirting of the question in
" The Prince d'Aurec," and " The Three Daughters of M. Dupont," compare the various-sided
treatment in each.

3. The use of letters and handkerchiefs and
veils has often been scoffed at as out of date,
" time-worn props from the arsenal of the inex-
haustible Scribe." Is the finding of the veil in
the last act of " The Pardon " skilfully introduced?

4. What is the " struggle " in this play? Is it
physical? Is the audience interested in this struggle, whatever it may be, in the characterization, or
in the story?

5. In three contemporary French plays—" Les
Tenailles " (The Nippers) by Hervieu, " Amoureuse " (The Loving Wife) by Porto-Riche, and
" The Pardon "—the idea of the strengthening of
the bond between husband and wife through the
fault of the one or the other and the ultimate for-
giveness of the one wronged, is made manifest. In
the Hervieu play, the husband learns long after
that his wife has had a lover, but the fact that
the wife has a child and is economically dependent
on her husband who cannot well leave them, serves
only as a closer link binding their union. In the
Porto-Riche play the very fact that the husband
forgives the " erring " wife, that he cannot give

her up, is in his own words a further bond welding them together.

In what way does Lemaître treat this theme? Is it the principal idea in the play? If not, then what is? (" The Nippers " is translated as " In Chains "; see p. 152, present volume. " Amoureuse " has not been translated. The original text is published by Ollendorff, Paris.)

HENRI LAVEDAN

Henri Lavedan, born of a middle-class but cultured family at Orléans in the year 1859, was more fortunate as to educational advantages than many of his contemporaries. He went to school at first in the neighborhood of Orléans, then at Paris, and was graduated soon after the close of the Franco-Prussian War, in 1871. He studied for the Law for a year, and then gave it up, feeling that he was not suited for the profession. He made his literary début with a number of clever and rather cynical dialogues, picturing for the most part the "flâneurs"—idle clubmen—of Parisian society. His first play was "One Family," produced at the Comédie Française in the early 'nineties. This was followed by what is probably his best-known and finest play, "The Prince d'Aurec." Lavedan excels in his character work, the best examples of which are to be found in the play just mentioned, as well as in "The Latest Fad" (Le Nouveau Jeu) and "The Marquis de Priola."

PLAYS

ONE FAMILY (1891).
THE PRINCE D'AUREC (1892).
THE TWO NOBILITIES (1894).
HIGH LIFE (1895).

CATHERINE (1898). New York by Annie Russell 1898.

THE LATEST FAD (1898).

THE OLD SPORT (1899).

THE MEDICI (1901).

THE MARQUIS DE PRIOLA (1902).

VARENNES (in collaboration with G. Lenôtre) (1904).

THE DUEL (1905).

> Produced in the United States by Mr. Otis Skinner 1906.

SIRE (1909).

> Also produced by Mr. Skinner 1911.

THE TASTE FOR VICE (1911).

THE KING'S FAVORITE (1913).

TO SERVE (1913).

PÉTARD (1914).

" The Prince d'Aurec " is translated by Barrett H. Clark ("Three Modern Plays from the French," Holt, 1914).

REFERENCES: "Three Modern Plays from the French " (Holt, 1914).

THE PRINCE D'AUREC

A comedy in three acts. First published 1892. Translated by Barrett H. Clark (Holt, 1914).

Many modern French writers have dealt with the question of the aristocracy of to-day; among the dramatists are notably François de Curel ("Les Fossiles "), Paul Bourget (" L'Emigré "), and finally Lavedan ("Le Prince d'Aurec," "Catherine," and " Les Deux Noblesses "). The present play, by reason of its detailed characterization, its wit, its truth to life, is probably the best work of its kind written during the past quarter-century.

1. Dumas fils once said that a play should contain " A painting, an ideal, a judgment." This comedy of Lavedan's certainly contains " a painting." Does it have " an ideal " and " a judgment "? As a painting compare it with Ibsen's " Hedda Gabler." In what respects does each of these plays fall under any of the headings mentioned above? Were the purposes, so far as they had purposes, of the authors in any way comparable?

2. " The Prince d'Aurec " is an admirable example of dramatic background. The Prince himself is the chief object of interest, but he cannot always occupy the center of the stage; the audience would weary of him. The dramatist must therefore provide relief, without that relief's causing our attention to swerve appreciably from the figure who must always remain at least near the foreground. His problem was how to divert us and yet tell something important about the Prince. This difficult feat of keeping the interest from flagging and yet keeping us amused is so well accomplished that we are scarcely aware that in those scenes where the Prince is absent, we are ever seeing the influences which have helped to make him what he is. If we are shown members of the *bourgeoisie*, like De Horn and Montade,

it is only that we shall contrast the born aristocrat with the born bourgeois; if we are amused at "Jojo's" sallies and the Duchess' "breaks," it is that the dramatist is furnishing legitimate amusement for us—but he is furnishing at the same moment sidelights on the Prince's character. The Prince might well have been a different man had it not been for the ambition and stupidity of his *parvenue* mother.

The play opens with a significant scene: creditors are pressing the Prince. Though we have not yet seen the man himself, we already know something of him. The scene likewise serves to arouse our curiosity: how will D'Aurec extricate himself from his pecuniary difficulties? When he finally enters, he is an object of interest. He is himself not long in arousing further interest. His summary disposal of the creditors we know will result in disaster later on. Throughout the play the author, with great skill, alternates scene with scene, with the hero and without him, but in each we learn something about him.

Are there any scenes in which the Prince ceases to develop? That is, is there a single superfluous scene in the play?

3. Why are Montade and De Horn so carefully elaborated? What is the purpose of the little scene between the Duchess and the lawyer who years previously asked her to become his wife?

MAURICE DONNAY

Maurice Donnay was born in 1854 at Paris, of a well-to-do middle-class family in the district of Montmartre. Although the young man early displayed a liking and some talent for literature, his parents wished him to become a civil engineer. Educated in his native city, he entered a contractor's office in 1885, where he remained for six years. Because he recited some verses of his own in a cabaret in Montmartre, he was forced to resign from his position. For two years he appeared at the " Chat Noir," where his graceful and satirical " saynètes "—little verses and dialogues—brought him considerable local popularity. In 1892, " Lysistrata," his first play, was produced at the Grand Théâtre. This adaptation of Aristophanes enjoyed some success, but the play which followed it, " Lovers," immediately gave him national fame. It has remained his best-known and best-loved play. Among Donnay's numerous plays, all of which deal in one manner or another with the relations of the sexes, the most typical are " The Other Danger," " The Sad Woman," and " The Return from Jerusalem."

PLAYS

LYSISTRATA (1892).
FAMILY HOTEL (1894).

LOVERS (1895).

THE SAD WOMAN (1897).

THE EMANCIPATED WOMAN (1898).

GEORGETTE LEMEUNIER (1898).

THE TORRENT (1899).

A PRINCE'S EDUCATION (1900).

THE CLEARING (in collaboration with L. Descaves) (1900).

THE SEESAW (1901).

THE OTHER DANGER (1902).

THE RETURN FROM JERUSALEM (1903).

Produced by Mme. Simone, United States, 1912-13.

THE ESCALADE (1904).

BIRDS OF PASSAGE (with L. Descaves) (1904).

TO APPEAR (1906).

THE PATRONESS (1908).

MOLIÈRE'S HOUSEHOLD (1912).

THE WOMEN SCOUTS (1913).

REFERENCES: *The Drama,* August, 1913; for " The Other Danger," " Three Modern Plays from the French " (Holt, 1914); " Lovers," " The Freed Woman," and " They," translated by Barrett H. Clark (Kennerley), 1915.

THE OTHER DANGER

A comedy in four acts. First published 1902. Translated by Charlotte Tenney David in " Three Modern Plays from the French " (Holt, 1914).

" The Other Danger " belongs to those plays of its author which treat in a serious manner the eternal problem of sex. This time the play is a study in

the struggle of the mother, with her lover and her
daughter. The colors are darker than Donnay as a
rule uses, but there is much in the work to recall the
charmingly sentimental author of " Lovers." It is
curious to watch this dramatist, who is as a rule not
preoccupied with theses, attacking one of the most
tragic of situations. The critic Jules Lemaître once
said that what brought Donnay closer to life than
most of his contemporaries was his comparative disregard of form. " The Other Danger " is not a " well-
made " play: it is hardly unified, and yet it is effective, and when it was produced, it enjoyed a considerable degree of success.

1. In what respects is " The Other Danger "
not a well-made play? Take act by act, and indicate where Donnay departs from the precepts
of Scribe and Sardou. Are his transgressions in
the nature of omissions or has he added material
which is from the standpoint of the perfect tech-
nician superfluous?

2. Could the entire first act be left out? If
it were, could the material therein contained be
placed, without serious prejudice to the author's
ideas and the play itself, in the exposition of
what is now the second act? Or might the first
and second acts be melted into one? What would
be lost by that process?

3. Some critics have urged that Donnay, feeling that his theme was repellent—which it is—

occupied as much time as possible in leading up to the climax. Is this true? Is Donnay more concerned with the play than the theme? If so, what are the proofs?

4. In this play, the author has pleased to show us Madeleine first at the age of twelve, then sixteen, then nearly eighteen. Ibsen's method would probably have been to show her only as the young lady who is looking for a husband—a " jeune fille à marier." Would Ibsen's catastrophic-drama process improve the French play, had Donnay chosen to adopt it? What is gained by his allowing us to see two stages in the girl's development, before the play, for her, really begins?

5. In the theater we must believe. If an author in a serious play—that is, in anything but a farce, in which he frankly asks us to assume certain impossibilities—fails to impress us with the fact that what is happening is so, the play will certainly fail to touch us. In the present play, can we believe, in spite of the clever and ingenious arguments brought forward by Freydières, that Madeleine cannot possibly do without him? Note carefully how the author attempts to make this situation credible.

6. There is a good deal of atmosphere created throughout the play, especially at the beginning of the first of its three acts. Much of this is not

pertinent to the plot and does very little toward
the development of character, but often there is
a clever welding of plot-progress and atmosphere.
Note in each instance how the various threads of
pertinent interest are woven into the " atmospheric " scenes.

HERVIEU

Paul Hervieu was born in 1857 at Neuilly, near Paris. He studied for the Bar, and passed his examinations at the age of twenty. After a few years' practice and after refusing a diplomatic post, he set to writing short stories and novels, which appeared in the early 'eighties. His first play, " Point de Lendemain," a short adaptation of a story, was produced in 1890, and five years later " The Nippers " appeared, firmly establishing Hervieu's reputation. He has continued to write for the stage, at the rate of one play in about every two years, and his latest play marks a distinct step in advance. He was elected to the French Academy in 1900.

The plays of Hervieu are perhaps the nearest approach to true tragedy of any of our time; they are also what the French call " thesis plays." With his faultless logic, clear and direct methods of writing, and admirable sincerity, he comments on and criticises those phases of life that seem to need correcting—the law, chiefly, and its relation to man and woman in the married state. " Les Tenailles " (The Nippers) is the story of a woman who tries to leave her husband and get a divorce; the husband refuses, until some years later his wife tells him, in a dispute, that he is not the father of the child. Whereupon she refuses to be divorced, in spite of her husband's insist-

ence. The child binds them together. "We are
only two miserable beings," she says, "and misery
knows none but equals." "La Course du Flambeau"
(The Passing of the Torch) shows the sacrifice of one
generation for the next; "Le Dédale" (The Labyrinth) proves the thesis that the child is the everlasting bond between man and wife. The best plays of
Hervieu—"Le Dédale," "Les Tenailles," "La
Course du Flambeau"—rightfully place their author,
in Mr. Huneker's words, as "the present master-psy-
chologist of the French stage."

PLAYS

POINT DE LENDEMAIN * (1890).

WORDS REMAIN (1892).

THE NIPPERS (1895).

THE LAW OF MAN (1897).

THE ENIGMA (1901).

Produced in New York by Miss Olga Nethersole.

THE PASSING OF THE TORCH (1901).

Produced in Chicago by The Drama Players, 1912.

THÉROIGNE DE MÉRICOURT (1902).

THE LABYRINTH (1903).

Produced in New York by Miss Nethersole 1905.

THE AWAKENING (1905). Given by Miss Nethersole.

MODESTY (one act) (1908).

KNOW THYSELF (1909).

Produced by Arnold Daly, New York, 1910.

BAGATELLE (1912).

* A proverbial expression meaning "without consequence," or "with no after-thought."

" The Nippers " is translated as " In Chains " by
Ysidor Asckenasy (*Poet-Lore*, 1909), and as " En-
chained " by the same (*The Dramatist*, 1910).
" The Labyrinth " is translated by Barrett H. Clark
and Lander MacClintock (Huebsch, 1913); and
" Modesty " by Barrett H. Clark (Samuel French,
1913).

REFERENCES: Huneker, " Iconoclasts "; Archer,
" Playmaking "; introduction to the translation of
" The Labyrinth."—*Magazines: International Re-
view,* vol. vii (p. 265); *Critic,* vol. xxxvii (p. 158).

THE LABYRINTH

A drama in five acts. First published 1903. Translated by Barrett H. Clark and Lander MacClintock.

1. " What is a tragedy? It is a play every
part of which aims to create suspense, deep thinking, and pity. It is accompanied no longer, as of
old, with magnificent draperies; it is a thing of the
day, logical, prosaic, no longer bloody . . . the
ways of Fate are no longer manifested, as with the
Greeks, in dreams, visions, or presentiments. Nowadays we try to show how the struggle for existence bears down inexorably upon those who are
imprudent, too weak to defend themselves, those
whose passions are stronger than their will
power." This is what M. Hervieu says about
tragedy; and this play is considered a good exam-

ple of such. Why? What is the tragic element
in the "Labyrinth"? With the author's own text
as a basis, we might infer that it is tragic because
(1) there was imprudence in the making of the
divorce laws of France, (2) because the people
concerned are, being human, too weak to defend
themselves, and (3) "their passions are stronger
than their will power."—The child inevitably
forms the binding link* between Max and Marianne, in spite of the fact that the two are entirely
incompatible; circumstances arise that make it impossible for these parents to live as man and wife.
What is to become of the child? The tragedy is
the child's tragedy, yet the mother is the greater
sufferer.

2. Francisque Sarcey, one of the greatest
French critics of the last century, brought into
current use a phrase which is quite untranslatable
but, as I shall point out, the meaning of which is
easy to show: "Scène à faire." Literally, a
"scene which is made necessary by the exigencies
of the plot." Archer † calls it the "Obligatory
scene," and this may be used as a good equivalent.
He says, "An obligatory scene is one which the
audience (more or less clearly and consciously)
foresees and desires, and the absence of which it

* The same theme is treated in Strindberg's "The Link"
and in Brieux's "La Berceau" (The Cradle).
  † "Playmaking," chap. xiii.

may with reason resent." In Henry Arthur
Jones's " Mrs. Dane's Defence," the examination
scene in the third act is the obligatory scene; in
the "Doll's House," it is the final conversation
between Nora and Torvald; in "A Gauntlet"
(second version), it is the final scene. It is
always the scene which if left out would occasion
a very noticeable breach. In "The Labyrinth,"
the obligatory scene is that between Max and Marianne, which ends the third act. This seems inevitable; it is moreover vital, logical, and, from
what had preceded it, to be expected. Not
perhaps the outcome, but the clash, the struggle.
One interesting question arises at this juncture:
Where is the climax? At the end of the third act
or the fourth?

That question may be answered by consulting
the last two acts. If these, the fourth at least,
keep up the suspense, and contain radically new
material, and if, beginning only with the fifth act,
the *dénouement*, or unraveling begins, then the
climax is at the end of the fourth. Does the
fourth act rise or fall? Does it picture the result
of the foregoing action, or does it carry on the un-
resolved action up to a still higher point? Determine that, and you will find the climax.

Returning to the obligatory scene question, look
for such scenes in the following plays: Pinero's
" His House in Order " and " Mid-Channel,"

Shaw's "Candida," and Rudolf Besier's "Don."
There are clearly defined *scènes à faire* in all of
these plays.

3. We have said that the *dénouement*, in most
cases the last act of a play, is the most difficult for
the dramatist. The weakest part of the "Labyrinth" is the last two acts. Most critics are not
satisfied with the solution, and they call M. Hervieu to task for disposing of Max and Guillaume
as he does. It is true that their death seems at
first a rather facile dramatic expedient, but it is
equally true that as yet there has been no satisfactory alternative suggested. One critic * thinks
it would be best to omit the last act. But this
would be too inconclusive; the audience ought to
have some hint as to the fate of the persons in
whom they have interested themselves. To leave
Marianne in her unbearable "labyrinth," and the
two men at each other's throats, would have been
highly unsatisfactory; yet it would be impossible
for Marianne to return to either Max or Guillaume. That is clear, and it would be equally impossible to kill Marianne, leaving the child to Max.
The men must be got out of the way, both of them.
That being the only possible solution of the problem, Hervieu has accomplished his task in a mas-
terly fashion. If you will conceive the situation,

* Paul Flat, in his second volume of "Figures du
Théâtre Contemporain" (Sansot, 1913).

you will see that Max and Guillaume are bound
sooner or later to meet, and that one will kill the
other.   But that would be worse yet; for either
the husband or the father of the child would survive.   Therefore, by killing both, the author has
merely compressed into a conclusive incident what
is possible, probable, and practically inevitable.

BRIEUX

Eugène Brieux, the son of a carpenter, was born in Paris in 1858. He showed an early liking for literature, and soon went into the field of journalism. He was for some years editor of the *Nouvelliste* at Rouen, and it was in that city that he wrote his earlier plays, sending them to Paris for production. One of the first of these, " Ménages d'Artistes," was accepted and produced by Antoine at the Théâtre Libre (1890) and two years later the same manager brought forth the young dramatist's first important success, " Blanchette." Returning to Paris, as soon as he could make a living there, he married and devoted himself to the writing of that series of plays to which he now owes his international fame. In 1910 he was made a member of the French Academy.

Brieux and Hervieu are the best exponents of the thesis play in France. Hervieu, we have seen, attacks certain phases of the law, especially those regarding the marriage relation. He attacks, however, in a cold and absolutely logical way, proving each step in his argument. Brieux attacks many institutions and prejudices; he declares * himself the enemy

* " . . . My method—if such it can be called—consists of crying out against every abuse of power. It is a fact that all forms of power, all authority, arouse my indigna-

of every " abuse of power " and all authority, for he
believes that men are too frail to sit in judgment over
their fellow-beings.   He attacks society because it
will not give young girls an opportunity of earning an
honest living by teaching (" Blanchette "); he lays
bare the evils of the political " system " (" The Machine "); of charity and its abuse (" The Philanthropists "); of science and its abuse (" The Eva-
sion "); of marriage arrangements (" The Three
Daughters of M. Dupont "); of the attitude of se-
crecy concerning the nature, effects, and cure of the
so-called unmentionable (venereal) diseases and ren-
ovates and brings to light the truth of the matter
(" Damaged Goods "); in the " Red Robe " he shows
how certain parts of the legal system are inherently
bad.   In " Maternity " he declares war on those who
fail to regard motherhood as sacred, something to be
protected for the good of the race.   In each play, he
criticises some aspect of a living question.   His purpose is always to treat in a sincere and direct manner
every plague-sore that he believes can be treated.
Of necessity he is often brutally outspoken; he must
be in order to make himself heard and believed.   He
says: * " We [the dramatists] must have an idea in our
plays . . . taken from the life about us, from among
the sufferings of our fellow-beings."

tion, because in human hands they develop sooner or later
into tyranny."   Extract from letter to the author, Jan. 5,
1912.

* In the *Revue Bleue,* quoted by Bertrand (E. Brieux,
Sansot, 1910).

PLAYS

Bernard Palissy (in collaboration with G. Salandri) (1880).

The Divorce Office (in collaboration with G. Salandri) (1880).

Artists' Families (1890).

Duramé's Daughter (1890).

M. de Réboval (not published) (1892).

Blanchette (1892). New York in French 1914.

The Brood (1893).

The Machine (1894).

The Blue Rose (one act) (1895).

The Philanthropists (1897).

The Escape (1897).

The Three Daughters of M. Dupont (1899).
   Produced by Laurence Irving in New York, and on
      tour 1910.

The School for Mothers-in-law (from "The
      Brood," one act) (1898).

Racing Results (1898).

The Cradle (1898).

The Red Robe (1900).
   Produced in New York in German 1903, in French
      by Réjane 1904.

The Substitutes (1901).

Damaged Goods (1902).
   Produced in a number of cities in America 1913-
      14 by Richard Bennett. Mr. Bennett first
      used the translation by John Pollock, later
      one by Benjamin F. Blanchard (unpublished).

The Little Friend (1902).

MATERNITY (1st version) (1904).

> (2nd version only in English 1911). New York 1915.

THE DESERTER (collaboration with Jean Sigaux (1904).

THE ARMATURE (dramatized from Hervieu's novel of the same name) (1905).

THE MAY BEETLES (Les Hannetons) (1906).

> Produced by Laurence Irving in New York 1909, first as "The Incubus" and later as "The Affinity."

THE FRENCHWOMAN (1907).

SIMONE (1908).

SUZETTE (1909).

FAITH (1912).

THE INDEPENDENT WOMAN (1912).

THE BOURGEOIS IN THE COUNTRY (1914).

"The Three Daughters of M. Dupont" translated by St. John Hankin; "Damaged Goods" by John Pollock; "Maternity" (first version) by Mrs. Bernard Shaw, and (second version) by John Pollock, published in a volume, "with a preface by Bernard Shaw" (Brentano, 1911); "Blanchette," and "The Escape" by Frederick Eisemann (Luce, 1913).

REFERENCES: Shaw's preface to "Three Plays by Brieux" (Brentano, 1911); "The Plays of Eugène Brieux" by P. V. Thomas (A. C. Fifield, London, 1913). *Magazines: Atlantic,* vol. xc (p. 79); *Contemporary Review,* vol. lxxxi (p. 343); *Forum,* vol.

xliii (p. 678); and vol. xlvii (p. 405); *Nation,* vol.
xciii (p. 149); *Drama,* August, 1913.

THE THREE DAUGHTERS OF
M. DUPONT

A comedy in four acts. First published 1899. Translated by St. John Hankin.

1. " The Three Daughters of M. Dupont " is
not Brieux's best play, but it is perhaps as truly
representative as anything he has written. The
good and bad qualities of this dramatist are more
apparent here than in almost any other of his
plays.

This is a thesis play par excellence; the author
wishes to demonstrate or prove a definite theme
or thesis. In the " Three Daughters of M. Dupont," he wishes to expose the evil side of the
present French system of marriage in its bearing
on women. There are three points which he makes
and he creates three characters, each illustrating
one point. Let us see how every side of the question is handled, and whether the author chooses to
suggest any solution to his problem, or merely to
show a state of affairs.

2. The exposition is concerned first with the case
of Caroline, and when we have received sufficient
information to enable us to distinguish her and her
story later, Julie enters. Notice how clearly (p.

82) these characters are drawn and differentiated one from the other. Caroline believes that Courthezon has succeeded in his invention " because she prayed for it," and Julie we learn has been to see Madame Leseigneur, for she only goes " to houses where there are children." These indications are followed by many others (pp. 82-83) until there is not the slightest danger that the audience will forget what it is needful they should have well in mind. The next character to be introduced is not the remaining daughter, but M. Dupont. Brieux might have brought Angèle in as a subject of conversation, but there are two reasons against this procedure: (1) Angèle is not usually mentioned within the family circle, and (2) the scene needed variety. The introduction or even the mention of a third daughter so early in the act, would tend to make the play even more diagrammatic than it is. Therefore we learn of the project to marry off Julie, and that the " intended's " parents, the Mairauts, are coming to arrange the marriage. Then (p. 90) Angèle is spoken of in a natural way, and her story told.—The formal proposal for Julie's hand occupies the rest of the first act.

3. When Bernard Shaw says * that " in that great comedy which Balzac calls the ' comedy of humanity,' to be played for the amusement of the gods rather than that of the French public, there is

* Preface to " Three Plays by Brieux."

no summit in the barren plain that stretches from
Mount Molière to our times until we reach Brieux,"
he must refer to such scenes as that (pp. 97-107)
in which the Mairauts and the Duponts make arrangements for their children's union. This particular scene recalls Molière and Labiche, and if he
had written no others should certainly entitle
Brieux to rank as a writer of true comedy.

Compare with scenes similarly treated, in Molière's " L'Avare " (The Miser) and Labiche's
" La Poudre aux Yeux " (Dust in the Eyes).

4. The second act brings us face to face with
Julie's tragedy ; this is *her* act. When she says to
her husband, " The real evil is that our parents
married us as they did marry us. . . . And
here we are chained to one another," the case of
Julie is nearly disposed of. And when, later on,
it is clear that because of the selfishness and sen-
suality of her husband she is not permitted to have
children, her tragedy is complete.

5. The subsequent acts are concerned with the
cases of Angèle, who was forced to leave the family because of a " youthful slip " and become a
prostitute in Paris, and of Caroline, who, because
of the dowry system has lost her chances of marriage.—Julie too has been disposed of. The last
act brings the story to a close—a pessimistic, cynical close. The lives of the two elder sisters are
over, their fate sealed ; Julie at least had a chance,

and we are given to understand that she will leave her husband later on, when she has an opportunity. " And since to pay for bread to eat and clothes to wear and a roof to cover me I must either give myself to a husband I hate or to a lover whom, perhaps, I may love, I choose the lover." With these words, Julie's chapter closes. The " happy ending," Julie's reconciliation with her husband, is the bitterest part of the play; Julie ostensibly returns to " duty," but she is determined to escape it as soon as she can.

The end of one of Brieux's earliest plays, " Blanchette," contains a similarly " happy " catastrophe: the eager young girl who refuses to marry a peasant in the first act, is in the last, owing to circumstances over which she has no control, forced to do so.

ROSTAND

Edmond Rostand, the most celebrated of modern French dramatists, was born in 1868, at Marseilles. His early schooling was received in his native city. He came to Paris and entered the Lycée Stanislas; after his graduation he studied law and received the degree of "licencié." His first work of any note was a volume of poems, "Les Musardises," which appeared in 1890. Although these refined and skilfully written verses attracted some little attention, the poet did not become well known for a few years to come. In 1894 his first play, with the exception of an unimportant one-act trifle, was produced at the Comédie Française; "Les Romanesques," by its charm and delicate satire, captivated the public and such particular and conservative critics as Sarcey and Lemaître. This little comedy was followed by "La Princesse Lointaine," which Sarah Bernhardt played in 1895; the same actress also produced another play, "La Samaritaine," two years later. By the middle of the year 1897, Rostand was recognized as a poet of some distinction and a writer of charming but by no means remarkable plays. By the end of that year he was famous in France and by the end of the following he was a world-wide celebrity. On December 26, 1897, "Cyrano de Bergerac," with Constant Coquelin

in the title rôle, was produced at the Porte St. Martin
Theater in Paris. "Cyrano" was the greatest success
of modern times. The critics were unanimous in their
praise; Emile Faguet, a careful and in some ways conservative critic, writes: "Mon Dieu! M. Rostand,
how deeply I appreciate the fact that you exist!"
"L'Aiglon," played by Bernhardt, appeared in 1900.
The following year the poet was elected to the French
Academy. Owing to ill-health he left soon after for
the South; there, near the Spanish border, he built his
villa, Arnaga, where he still resides.—Since 1902, re-
ports were current to the effect that a new play, to be
called "Chantecler," was in preparation. After in-
numerable delays, due to author, actors, and managers, and owing further to the death of Coquelin, who
was to have played the principal part, "Chantecler"
did not appear until February, 1910. The play had
been too much advertised, and in consequence the
audience on the first night was disappointed and not
a little puzzled. The production was not a great
success financially, though most of the critics thought
it in no way inferior to the earlier works.—A little
later (April 20, 1910) Bernhardt produced "Le Bois
Sacré," a pantomime accompanied by a poem.

M. Rostand has been hailed as the prophet of a
great Romantic revival, but since he has no important
followers, it is as well to consider his work independently. He is, like Maeterlinck, of no school; he
has, or had—up to the production of "Chantecler"—
unlike Maeterlinck, no very distinct philosophy of life.
His plays are poetic, romantic, charming, and witty;

his is a healthy, human view of life. In " Chantecler " he paints his ideal: devotion, faith, love.

PLAYS

THE RED GLOVE (1888).
  (Not published.)
THE TWO PIERROTS (1891).
  (Not published.)
THE ROMANCERS (1894).
  Produced in New York at a matinée, in German
    1904-5.
THE PRINCESS FARAWAY (1895).
  Produced in New York as " My Lady of Dreams "
    by Mme. Simone 1912.
THE WOMAN OF SAMARIA (1897).
  Produced in New York by Mme. Bernhardt 1911.
CYRANO DE BERGERAC (1897).
  First produced in New York in English by Rich-
    ard Mansfield 1897, in French by Coquelin and
    Bernhardt 1900, in German 1898-9.
L'AIGLON (1900).
  First produced in New York in English by Maude
    Adams 1900, in French by Bernhardt and Coque-
    lin 1900.
CHANTECLER (1910).
  Produced in the United States by Maude Adams
    1910.
THE SACRED WOOD (1910).

" The Romancers " is translated by Mary Hender
(Doubleday, Page, 1899), by George Fleming as
" The Fantasticks " (Heinemann); there is also a

prose translation published by Samuel French; "The Princess Faraway" by Charles Renauld (Stokes, 1899); "Cyrano de Bergerac" by Gertrude Hall (Doubleday, Page, 1898), by Gladys Thomas and M. F. Guillemand (R. H. Russell, 1900), by Charles Renauld (Stokes, 1898), by Howard Thayer Kingsbury (1898), and by Helen B. Dole (New York, n.d.); "L'Aiglon" by Louis N. Parker (R. H. Russell, 1900); "Chantecler" by Gertrude Hall (Duffield, 1900).

REFERENCES: E. E. Hale, Jr., "Dramatists of Today"; Augustin Filon, "Modern French Drama" (Chapman and Hall, 1898), and G. K. Chesterton, "Five Types" (Holt, 1911).—*Magazines: Arena,* vol. xxxiv (p. 225); *North American Review,* vol. clxxii (p. 794); *Critic,* vol. xxxix (p. 437); *Edinburgh Review,* vol. cxcii (p. 307); *McClure's,* vol. xiv (p. 437). For bibliography, see "Modern Drama and Opera: A Reading List" (Boston Book Co., 1911).

CYRANO DE BERGERAC

A heroic comedy in five acts. First published 1897.
Translations indicated above.

1. "Cyrano de Bergerac" is one of the most celebrated of modern plays; no drama of the past twenty years has met with such unquestioned success. And this success may justly be attributed to its splendid characterization of the protagonist and its perfect realization of the spirit of romance.

The poetry is not a prime factor, for the play has succeeded in many translations.

The exposition is a triumph ; it would be difficult to name another play in which the period, the historical " milieu " are so deftly brought before us. Compare by way of contrast, the wholly adequate but cold and direct exposition of " Hedda Gabler."

Closely allied to the subject of exposition, and often a part of it, is the question of the first entrance of the principal character.   This is usually placed some minutes after the rise of the curtain in the first act, because (1) the attention required to grasp the main facts of the exposition must not be diverted by the appearance of the " star," (2) the " star " must be prepared for, and (3) he—or she—must appear at an effective moment.*   Avoiding the conventional entrance—as, for instance, a dramatic appearance at the back of the stage— Rostand brings in Cyrano unperceived and finally, when it is feared that he is absent, a voice from the multitude shouts, "Rascal, have I not forbidden you to appear for a month?"   Soon "a hand holding a cane rises up over the heads of the spectators," then " the cane is shaken," and at length Cyrano " stands up suddenly, standing on a chair, his arms crossed, his beaver cocked fiercely, his

* Compare the opening acts of Dumas fils' " La Dame aux Camélias " (Camille), Pinero's " The Second Mrs. Tanqueray," Shaw's " Candida," and Besier's " Don."

moustache bristling, his nose terrible to see." A novel entrance and very effective because of its utter unexpectedness, both to the audience on the stage and to that in the theater.

2. In all Rostand's plays are to be found long and elaborate speeches, tirades, that serve as veritable " *tours de force* " for the actors who recite them; the best of these are in " Cyrano," " L'Aiglon," and " Chantecler." In the first and last of these the speeches were written for Coquelin, in the second for Bernhardt. That is to say, they were deliberately intended for these actors because of their ability to declaim them in a highly effective manner.

Every play is a collaboration. There can be no play without actors, and the actors are of little use without a play. M. Rostand, like most dramatists, writes for his actors, with one eye of course on the audience; in this connection, Coquelin and Bernhardt have been of invaluable service to him. Coquelin was perfectly aware of his own powers and shortcomings, and the poet wrote more or less to order, to fit; Coquelin could deliver long speeches full of bravado, humorous and pathetic, and such speeches did Rostand write for him. Coquelin, in " Cyrano," wanted a death scene, and a death scene was prepared for him. In " L'Aiglon," Bernhardt wanted tirades and she wished to die; Rostand provided what was needful.—This collaboration is extremely helpful for author and actor, and in the cases we are now considering, quite justifiable and completely successful. Shakspere did the same thing, and practically every modern dramatist, especially the Americans of the present day, has at least the actor or actress in view whom he wishes to interpret the principal characters in his play. In certain of the plays of Henry Arthur Jones—" Mrs. Dane's Defence," " The Liars," " The Case of Rebellious Susan "—there are rôles known as " Wyndham " rôles, written especially for Sir Charles; many of Sardou's plays—" La Tosca," " Théodora," " Gismonda," " Cléopâtre," " La Sorcière " (The Sorceress)—were written to order for Bernhardt; most of Clyde Fitch's plays were written for particular actresses— " The Truth " for Clara Bloodgood, " Her Own Way " for Maxine Elliott, and " The Stubbornness of Geraldine " for Mary Mannering. Owing to the " star " system in America, it is often the case that the public comes to speak of " Mrs. Fiske's play " or " Otis Skinner's," rather than that of the author.*—But collaboration may have

* The practice is so common in this country that a few random instances will suffice: Augustus Thomas has found in John Mason one of his finest interpreters, and the principal rôles in " The Witching Hour " and " As a Man Thinks " might well be called Mason parts. Edward Sheldon has done much the same thing for Mrs. Fiske, in " Salvation Nell " and " The High Road."

a disastrous effect on both collaborators: the play may suffer because of over-emphasis on the principal character and the actor place too much importance upon himself and his rôle. Sardou was a poorer dramatist because of his association with Bernhardt, while that actress, great as she is, was led to sacrifice the play to her own individuality, to the detriment of both the play and, to a lesser extent, her own art. Richard Mansfield ruined many good plays—" Julius Cæsar " among them—because he considered that Richard Mansfield was more important than the work he was supposed to interpret.

3. " Cyrano " is a richly varied and highly elaborated work; the great number of scenes and huge cast constitute a picture of great extent. But there is unity throughout, in the figure of Cyrano. When he is not on the stage the memory of him remains, a speech or a " gesture," and if we are not thinking of what he did last we are looking forward to what he will do next.

Take the scenes—like that which opens the second act,—and discover in what way the author keeps the figure of Cyrano in the minds of the audience.

4. One of the laws of dramatic technique—it has many exceptions—is, Never keep a secret from the audience. The reason for this is clear: an

audience has only a little over two hours to enjoy
the foreshortened events of perhaps a lifetime, and
curiosity, pure and simple, plays too unimportant
a part in their evening's entertainment. If a secret is long withheld from them,* they become im-
patient. Paul Hervieu's "The Enigma" keeps a
secret to the end, and when it is known, there is
nothing but the solution to satisfy us; the time
spent in wondering who is guilty (one of two
women is unfaithful to her husband) might much
better have been employed in the enjoyment of
character delineation. Charles Lamb's play "Mr.
H." kept the mystery of its hero's name until the
very last, and when the revelation is made—his
name is Hogsflesh—there is little satisfaction.
Further, when once an audience learns the secret—
as they did in the case of Lamb's play after the
first night—the element of surprise, upon which
the play is based, is gone.

Little surprises and unforeseen events, however,
are quite legitimate; the long-lost relative, the dis-
covery of a forgotten letter, may be used with im-
punity—if any one should dare to employ such
relics of "Sardoodledom" in this sophisticated
age!—and they were unquestionably dramatic in
their day. The point to be borne in mind is that

* See Archer, "Playmaking," chap. xvii ("Keeping a
Secret"), and the same critic's article, "The God-like Play-
goer," *London Morning Leader,* September 24, 1910.

these little surprises are pleasant, and quite legitimate, so long as they do not interfere with the more serious business of the plot or characterization. In Jules Verne's " Tour of the World in 80 Days " (the dramatization, which was lately revived in Paris; one of the most popular plays of the last century) there is a splendid instance of surprise: the eighty days are up, and Fogg has apparently lost his wager. At the last moment he learns that he has gained a day in his tour, because of his race " with the sun,"—a fact forgotten by him and by the audience; the surprise is genuine and the pleasure spontaneous. In " Cyrano " (Act IV) Roxane's entrance is quite unexpected and is a surprise, but as her coming is not of prime importance, and as her identity is not long hidden, there is practically no curiosity, only a momentary surprise. These are examples where the audience is kept in ignorance, and is really surprised; their attention is not forced away from the play itself, and consequently it does not suffer. If, however, a secret is kept from the *characters*, but is known to the audience, our enjoyment is the greater. We in the audience know that Hamlet is going to fail: it is foreordained, and we know that Œdipus will struggle in vain against the decrees of Fate— but neither Hamlet nor Œdipus is aware of his impending tragedy. That knowledge on the part of the audience gives them the feeling of superiority of which Mr. Archer speaks, and makes each individual a " God-like Spectator."

5. Why should Cyrano die? The play is called a " heroic comedy," and yet it ends in death. First, it might be urged that Coquelin wished a part in which he could die, but Rostand is too great an artist to spoil his play for the sake of the personal desire to please even so distinguished an actor as his friend Coquelin. Further, the death of Cyrano is hardly an ordinary death; it is rather the apotheosis of his heroic life. He was ever unlucky, it was his life to " be the prompter—and be forgotten," and his death is a fitting end to his life; and yet—and this consoles us for his death— he bears away " unsmirched " his " panache "—his plume: the symbol of his honor.

Still, is the death of Cyrano logical? If Rostand had had free sway would he have killed his hero?

When he came to write " Chantecler," and portray a character similar to that of Cyrano, he let him live and triumph.

CHANTECLER

A play in four acts. First published 1910. Translated by Gertrude Hall.

When " Chantecler " appeared, the verdict seemed to be that it was not up to the author's standard, and it was not so great a success as most of the earlier plays. To the public the play was confusing. This was largely due to the symbolism and partly to the very brilliant quality of its style, which was more involved and much more difficult than that used in any of the other plays. But the critics * have for the most part by now agreed that " Chantecler " is in no way inferior to " Cyrano " and " L'Aiglon."

It is certainly superior to these plays in that it offers a criticism of life; it deals with human aspirations and struggles, and is not primarily concerned with a story. It is a modern play, the only one Rostand ever wrote, and marks an epoch in his spiritual and artistic development; it proves that during the ten years between the production " L'Aiglon " and that of " Chantecler " he was thinking about humanity. In that the poetry is as inspired as that of " Cyrano " and " L'Aiglon "— in spite of the " occasional faults " of which M.

---

* Emile Faguet, in a letter to the author, says, " Chantecler appears to me to be a work, in general, of high and noble inspiration. There is a constant aspiration toward the sublime. Certain parts, like the *Hymn to the Sun* and Chantecler's *Profession of Faith,* are full of great lyrical beauty, in spite of occasional faults. The bad qualities of the play are that it is too long, too ' filled out,' that there is too much ' *preciosity,*' too much wit, too many jokes, puns, plays on words, etc. Altogether, it is a very interesting work, quite worthy of . . . its author. . . ." (Paris, August, 1910).

Faguet speaks—" Chantecler " is because of its deeper ethical import, and its clearer insight into human character, Rostand's finest achievement.

In brief, " Chantecler " is, in the author's own words, the " drama of human endeavor grappling with life."

1. There arises first the question, Has the poet selected the very best medium of expression for his ideas? Rostand has so well answered this question and explained his intentions, that I shall merely quote his words in full :* " I wished to write a modern play in verse. Now the lyrical qualities of a poetic production do not go well with the modern suit and the commonplace frock coat. It needs the additional costume. One must turn back for this two or three centuries, at least, or be obliged to set the play in countries of which the customs, language, and interests are very far from our own. But a poet may have the desire to express modern ideas with a modern vocabulary, to allude to happenings of the day the most Parisian, to laugh as one laughs on the boulevard in 1910, and to think as one thinks in France in the twentieth century. A problem difficult to solve! The sight of my barnyard at Cambo immediately offered me a solution. Why, here was the costume dreamt of,— if one can say so!—here indeed was the means of

* Quoted from "The Story of Chantecler," by Marco F. Liberma (Moffat, Yard, 1910).

remaining modern, and at the same time that of being picturesque and lyrical. Characters garbed in animal dress, expressing themselves like human beings,—like the Parisians of the day. What a find! And furthermore, what an opportunity to speak of things in nature, to be deeply moved by flowers, birds, the bits of grass, or the insect—and what a setting!—No, really, the poet could not wish for a more beautiful theme! "

2. With the above justification of the use of his medium, it is useless for us to discuss the question further. In order to do what Rostand wished to do, his adoption of it was the only course open to him. Let us see how he has succeeded. The play contains nothing very novel in technical treatment; its merits are largely lyrical and poetic. As we are concerned here mainly with the technical side of the question, we shall inquire into how the author has done his work, built his play, and developed his ideas.

The exposition is somewhat helped by the Prelude, or prologue: this creates atmosphere. It is indeed almost wholly " atmospheric." The exposition proper then merely adds to and rounds out the " milieu," and then introduces the characters. Note that there is practically nothing in the past that needs to be known, that the action starts on the stage, before our eyes. The Turkey and the Blackbird are soon sketched out, then Chantecler

comes, sings his Hymn to the Sun: Patou sounds
the note of warning and foreshadows Chantecler's
struggle, sowing seeds of doubt in his mind. The
Pheasant Hen arrives, Chantecler is captivated by
her brilliant plumage, and the love motif has begun. There remains only the setting in motion
of the wheels of action—the opposing forces;—
these opposing forces are the birds of the night,
together with the Blackbird, all conspiring against
Chantecler.—What will happen to him?

3. Of the themes announced in the first act, two
are developed in the second: the conspiracy
against Chantecler and the love of Chantecler and
the Pheasant Hen.—Chantecler voices his profession of faith to her, and tells her eventually his
secret. Then further threads are stretched for
additional acts to tangle and tighten, and later
unravel.

4. The third act is an elaborate exposition of
the fatuousness of the enemies of Chantecler.
Chantecler is the poet, the worker, the embodiment
of all that is best in the French nation, and his
enemies are the " Blagueurs," the faddists, the
philistines. The " Guinea-hen's Reception " is
the height of faddism; into the midst of this comes
the real enemy of Chantecler, the mercenary who
will overcome him by mere physical force. The
fight between the two is the climax of the play, and
Chantecler's triumphant moment—when he pro-

tects the barnyard against the Hawk—its culminating point.—But he must leave his old barnyard,
" to save his soul." The struggle is over, and the
opposing forces, chief among them the fighting
cock who in a fury cut one claw with the other,
are vanquished.—There remains now only the *dénouement*. What will Chantecler do? How will
his love for the Pheasant Hen end? The last act,
we know, will answer these questions.

5. The Pheasant Hen's jealousy of Chantecler's power, and his own idea that his song causes
the sun to rise, lead her to put Chantecler's faith
to the test. The momentary disillusion is a bitter
disappointment, for the sun rises independently of
Chantecler's " Cocorico! ", it is also cruel for him
to hear a voice sweeter than his own, that of the
Nightingale, but his faith in himself and his own
small mission, and finally that he is worth the sacrifice of the Pheasant Hen, renew his self-confi-
dence, and leave him bigger and stronger than he
was in his earlier and parochial surroundings, the
unquestioned lord of the little barnyard which was
but a small and unimportant corner of the world.

MAETERLINCK

Maurice Maeterlinck was born of a Flemish family
of ancient descent, at Ghent, Belgium, in 1862. In
accordance with the wishes of his parents he studied
for the law, and practised for some time after his
graduation, in his native city. But in 1886 he left Belgium for Paris, and there formed the acquaintance of
some writers who were later to exercise considerable
influence over him; among these was Villiers de L'Isle
Adam. He it was, according to Maeterlinck, directed
him "toward the spiritual, poetic, and mysterious
side of things." In 1889, after his return to Belgium
on the death of his father, he published his first
works, a volume of poems —" Serres Chaudes "—and
the " Princesse Malcine," a play which called forth
the extravagant praise of Octave Mirbeau, who called
its author " A Belgian Shakspere." Until 1896 he
spent most of his time in Belgium writing plays, a few
poems, and making translations from the English.
In that year he returned to Paris, leaving Belgium
permanently. From then on he has devoted himself
to his life-work, which comprises a number of philosophical works, the best-known of which are " Wisdom
and Destiny," " The Treasure of the Humble," " The
Buried Temple," and " The Life of the Bee."

Maeterlinck, although he writes in French, does not

belong to what is loosely termed the French school of dramatists; * he is a writer singularly apart and independent. He is in some respects the disciple of Poe and Emerson, both of whom played an important part in his development. Judging from some of his works, he might be classified as a Symbolist; yet, considering his total output, he is of no school. He occupies a unique position in modern drama and literature, as playwright, mystic, symbolist, and philosopher. Briefly, he has tried to express moods, sub-conscious and half-realized feelings, and in order to do so he has created the so-called " Static " drama, the drama of situation and atmosphere.

In " The Treasure of the Humble " he makes clear his position regarding this new form: " I have grown to believe that an old man, seated in his armchair, waiting patiently, with his lamp beside him; giving unconscious ear to all the eternal laws that reign about his house, interpreting, without comprehending, the silence of doors and windows and the quivering voice of the light, submitting with bent head to the presence of his soul and his destiny—an old man who conceives not that all the powers of this world, like so many heedful servants, are mingling and keeping vigil in his room, who suspects not that the very sun itself is supporting in space the little

* Unfortunately, the great mass of representative French drama is still untranslated. Because of their inaccessibility to English readers, such important dramatists as Capus, Bernstein, and Bataille, are not represented in the present volume.

The *Drama*, however, will soon publish a play of Capus.

table against which he leans, or that every star in heaven and every fiber of the soul are directly concerned in the movement of an eyelid that closes, or a thought that springs to birth—I have grown to believe that he, motionless as he is, does yet live in reality a deeper, more human, and more universal, life than the lover who strangles his mistress, the captain who conquers in battle, or 'the husband who avenges his honor.'"

Maeterlinck's later development has made necessary a modification of the statement that his chief contribution to the modern drama is the invention of the Static play. He himself realizes the futility of the pigeon-holing system in literature, and in a letter to the author * makes clear his own ideas on the subject: "You must not attach too great importance to the expression 'Static'; it was an invention, a theory of my youth, worth what most literary theories are worth—that is, almost nothing. Whether a play be *static*, or *dynamic, symbolistic,* or *realistic,* is of little consequence. What matters is that it be well written, well thought out, human and, if possible, superhuman, in the deepest significance of the term. The rest is mere rhetoric." Maeterlinck is perhaps a little too modest, but this statement is only a further proof of his own development.

* Dated, Nice, 8 November, 1913.

PLAYS

THE PRINCESS MALEINE (1889).

THE BLIND (1890).

> Produced in New York by Sargent's American
> Academy of Dramatic Arts 1908.

THE INTRUDER (1890).

> Produced in New York by Sargent's American
> Academy of Dramatic Arts 1909.

THE SEVEN PRINCESSES (1891).

PELLÉAS AND MÉLISANDE (1892).

> Produced in New York as a play by Mrs. Patrick
> Campbell 1902, and in operatic form with De-
> bussy's music by Hammerstein 1908.

ALLADINE AND PALOMIDES (1894).

INTERIOR (1894).

THE DEATH OF TINTAGILES (1894).

> First Produced in New York by Julius Hoppe's
> Progressive Stage Society; later at a matinée, by
> Sargent's American Academy of Dramatic Arts
> 1914.

AGLAVAINE AND SÉLYSETTE (1896).

ARDIANE * AND BARBE-BLEUE (1901).

> Produced in New York as an opera with Dukas's
> music 1911.

SISTER BEATRICE (1901).   In English New York
> 1912.   In French by Sarah Bernhardt.

MONNA VANNA (1903).

> Produced in New York, 1903, by Bertha Kalisch.
> In Boston as opera with Février's music 1913.

---

* This spelling is that of the authorized translation.   In
the original the name is spelled " Ariane."

JOYZELLE (1903).

THE BLUE BIRD (1908).

Produced at the New Theater, New York, 1910.

MARY MAGDALENE (1913).*

Produced at the New Theatre, New York, by Olga
Nethersole 1911.

"The Princess Maleine" is translated by Gerard
Harry (Heinemann, 1892), by Richard Hovey (Stone
and Kimball, 1894; Duffield, 1906; (Dodd, Mead,
1911); "The Blind" by Richard Hovey (Dodd,
Mead, 1911), and as "The Sightless" by Laurence
Alma-Tadema (Scott, London, n.d.); "The Intruder"
by William Wilson (Heinemann, 1892) and by Richard Hovey (Dodd, Mead, 1911); "The Seven Princesses" by Richard Hovey (Dodd, Mead, 1911), and
by Charlotte Porter and Helen A. Clarke (*Poet-Lore,*
1894); "Pelléas and Mélisande" by Laurence Alma-
Tadema (Scott, London, n.d.), by Charlotte Porter
and Helen A. Clarke (*Poet-Lore,* 1894), and by Richard Hovey (Dodd, Mead, 1911); "Alladine and Palomides" by Alfred Sutro (Gowans and Gray, London,
1911) and by Richard Hovey (Dodd, Mead, 1911);
"Interior," as "Home" by Richard Hovey (Dodd,
Mead, 1911); "The Death of Tintagiles" by Alfred
Sutro (Gowans and Gray, 1911), and by Richard
Hovey (Dodd, Mead, 1911); "Aglavaine and Sély-
sette" by Alfred Sutro (Dodd, Mead, 1911), and in
Poet-Lore, 1909; "Ardiane and Barbe-bleue" by
Bernard Miall (Dodd, Mead, 1902); "Sister Bea-

* The English translation appeared in 1910; the French
original in 1913.

trice" by Bernard Miall (Dodd, Mead, 1902);
"Monna Vanna" by Alfred Sutro (Dodd, Mead,
1907), by A. I. duP. Coleman (Harpers, 1904), and
in *Poet-Lore;* "Joyzelle" by Clarence Stratton
(*Poet-Lore,* 1905), and by A. Teixeira de Mattos
(Dodd, Mead, 1907); "The Blue Bird" by Alexander Teixeira de Mattos (Dodd, Mead, 1909—with
an additional act, 1912); "Mary Magdalene" by
Alexander Teixeira de Mattos (Dodd, Mead, 1910).

In the United States Dodd, Mead and Co. publish
translations of the complete dramatic works. "Alladine and Palomides," "Interior," and "The Death
of Tintagiles" are included in one volume (Gowans
and Gray, 1911), with an introduction by H. Granville Barker. Nearly all the above translations contain introductions, with much valuable biographical
and critical matter.

REFERENCES: Montrose J. Moses, "Maurice Mae-
terlinck: A Study" (Duffield, 1911); Edward
Thomas, "Maurice Maeterlinck" (Dodd, Mead,
1911); shorter studies in: W. L. Courtney, "The
Development of Maurice Maeterlinck, and Other
Sketches of Foreign Writers" (Richards, 1904); Ash-
ley Dukes, "Modern Dramatists"; E. E. Hale, Jr.,
"Dramatists of To-day"; Archibald Henderson,
"Interpreters of Life and the Modern Spirit" (Ken-
nerley, 1905); James Huneker, "Iconoclasts";
Arthur Symons, "The Symbolist Movement in Litera-
ture" (Heinemann, 1900); Edwin Björkman,
"Voices of To-morrow" (Kennerley, 1913); Maurice
Maeterlinck, "The Modern Drama" (in his "The

Double Garden," Dodd, Mead, 1904).—*Magazines:*
Mme. Maeterlinck, in *Fortnightly,* vol. xciii (p. 48).
Moses's " Life," and " Modern Drama and Opera:
A Reading List " (Boston Book Co., Boston, 1911),
contain extensive bibliographies.

THE INTRUDER

A play in one act. First published 1890. Translated by Richard Hovey.

1. This little play is one of the most striking
examples of the " atmosphere " drama of modern
times. Maeterlinck's object is to create the feeling of the approach of death; death is the protagonist, the principal character, and although it
never appears on the stage, it is the most important " character " in the play.

The Modern Drama is the drama of exceptions,
for few rules can apply to any great portion of it.
In " The Intruder " there is no struggle, only a
mood; there is little development and practically
no action. It is a " static " drama of mood.

2. We have seen how dialogue should advance
the plot, or reveal character, or—to a lesser extent
—create atmosphere. In this play it rather tells
what plot there is and merely sketches the principal characters; but for the most part it is employed to create atmosphere. When the Father
(p. 10, Dodd, Mead edition) says, " We need have
no more anxiety. She is out of danger—" the

speech is purely exposition of fact or opinion, without further embellishment; when the Uncle (p. 11) says, "You know quite well your father-in-law likes to alarm us needlessly," he tells us something of the character of the Grandfather; and when (p. 20) the Grandfather says, "It seems to me that the cold comes into the room," and the Daughter answers, "There is a little wind in the garden, grandfather, and the rose leaves are falling," that is atmosphere, pure and simple. Those lines create a mood and they have very little to do either with plot or character.

3. Distinguish between the speeches which create atmosphere and those which do not.

PELLÉAS AND MÉLISANDE

A play in five acts. First published 1892. Translated by Richard Hovey, Charlotte Porter, and Helen A. Clarke; and Laurence Alma-Tadema.

1. "Pelléas and Mélisande" is the first of Maeterlinck's plays to contain a distinct and well-developed plot. "The Princess Maleine" was a phantasmagoria, disjointed and obscure; "The Intruder," "The Blind," and "The Seven Princesses" were "Static" mood-pictures without stories. "Pelléas and Mélisande," besides showing a great advance in plot construction, contains unmistakable indications of development of the

power to delineate character. What were mere
marionettes in the earlier plays, so strange and
far-away that they could evince little else than
wonder, in this play become flesh and blood.
Mélisande is a human being, and our sympathies
are aroused by her misfortunes.

1. This play is a turning point in the dramatic career of the author. He realizes that the
drama cannot be static and living at once, he
feels the shortcomings of his earlier efforts.

In order fully to understand this progress the
student must note carefully what parts of " Pelléas and Mélisande " belong to the " early " period,
and what are new. Compare " The Intruder "
with the present play, and note wherein the later
differs from it. Then, in connection with " Monna
Vanna," note the greater care taken to draw character than in " Pelléas and Mélisande."

In " The Intruder " do you find any external
incident, important in and for itself, which would
be visible in a stage representation ; rather than as
a mere indication of what is going on in the mind
of the character? What scenes in " Pelléas and
Mélisande " are independent of the rest of the
play, interesting and effective?

In " The Blue Bird " do you notice any technical advance over " Pelléas and Mélisande "?
Over Monna Vanna?

2. This play is so evanescent in mood, so sat-

urated with romance, that it suffers from analysis. The suggestions here given should therefore be carried out only after a complete and sympathetic reading. Like most of Maeterlinck's plays, it is more interesting as a study of atmosphere, an evocation of the subconscious self, than as acted drama.

Lamb once remarked that "King Lear" was too great to be played; an old man in a false beard, his ravings accompanied by rumblings of thunder made by beating upon a sheet of tin, could not but spoil the effect of transcendent greatness produced by a reading of the play. The case of Maeterlinck is somewhat analogous. One false note struck by an actor in a play like "The Intruder" or "Pelléas and Mélisande" might spoil the effect of the entire scene. Many scenes in "The Blue Bird," even in the well-intentioned productions in America and France, were nearly ruined; the moment "The Land of Memory" is put on the stage (and the "set" designed for the Art Theater of Moscow is thoroughly adequate) Maeterlinck's "Land of Memory," the one created in the imagination of the intelligent reader, vanishes. "The Kingdom of the Future," as played by children and women acting as children, often verges on the ridiculous.

Some plays suffer from presentation. Are they, then, plays? According to our definition, a play must be presented by actors on a stage, before an audience. We must conclude that such works as "Pelléas and Mélisande" and "The Blue Bird" are plays, but that the art of acting and stage management is not yet able to cope with certain problems, in spite of the splendid pioneer work of Gordon Craig, Max Reinhardt, Stanislavsky, and Meyerkhold—the last two, directors of the Art Theater of Moscow.*

MONNA VANNA

A play in three acts. First published 1903. Translated by Alfred Sutro.

In "Monna Vanna" Maeterlinck entered the realm of the actual acting drama.† He had formerly held that action was not necessary for a play, but, influenced either by his own experience or by the actress Georgette Leblanc—now Madame Maeterlinck—he declares that "There are no words

---

* Numerous designs and plans of new theaters and new methods of stage management are to be found in "L'Art Théâtral Moderne," par Jacques Rouché (Edouard Cornély, Paris, 1910). See also "Die Revolution des Theaters," Georg Fuchs (Georg Müller, Leipzig and München, 1909), and "The New Spirit in Drama and Art" by Huntley Carter (Palmer, London, 1913).

† Maeterlinck himself realizes this change of attitude; in a letter to the author (Nice, November, 1911), he speaks of "Pelléas et Mélisande" as being in his "first" and "Monna Vanna" his "second manner."

so profound, so noble and admirable, but they will soon weary us if they leave the situation unchanged, if they lead to no action, bring about no decisive conflict, or hasten no definite solution." *

1. In this play, then, there is a very definite struggle, one of the eternal struggles, that between love and duty. But the interest lies largely in the central figure, in the character of Monna Vanna. She is the first complete full-length portrait in the plays of Maeterlinck. The plot, background, and struggle are therefore employed only as a means of letting us know more of her, to bring to light further and deeper knowledge of the inmost recesses of her spiritual being. The sacrifice which she is called upon to make, for instance, reveals what may be termed her " civic conscience," her renunciation of personal happiness for the good of her people; each act will be found to test her mind and heart, and each scene in which she appears adds to our knowledge of her. It is she who interests us, not the situations in which she figures. There is what may seem a contradiction of this in the second act, in the tent scene. Suspense adds greatly to the interest of the scene; we are of course anxious to see how the scene will end, but we are more anxious to see how Monna Vanna will act, and what effect Prinzivalle will produce

* Quoted by Montrose J. Moses, " Maurice Maeterlinck: A Study," p. 119.

upon her, and what effect she upon him. The scene is skilfully managed, in that dramatic suspense and character delineation are so interwoven that we are scarcely aware which is which; it is only after a somewhat detailed analysis that we can distinguish the component elements.

2. To a lesser extent Maeterlinck discusses morality in his play; this is outside the strict confines of the present study, but it may be interesting to note what Arthur Symons (in " Plays, Acting, and Music ") has to say on the subject: " Here is a play in which almost every character is noble, in which treachery becomes a virtue, a lie becomes more vital than truth, and only what we are accustomed to call virtue shows itself mean, petty, and even criminal.   And it is most like life, as life really is, in this: that at any moment the whole course of the action might be changed, the position of every character altered, or even reversed, by a mere decision of the will, open to each, that the choice could be otherwise."

3. The climax occurs, as might have been expected, at the end of the second act, but note that the third is remarkably well sustained.   The tension is by no means released as the curtain rises for the last time; we must know how Guido will receive his wife on her return.   The scene we expect is a " scène à faire," not the " scène à faire " (that was in the preceding act) but a lesser one; it is

eagerly awaited, and we should have reason for
complaint against the dramatist were we deprived
of it. Notice how suspense is created and sustained: the crowd is in great excitement as their
savior enters the city, and this excitement is com-
municated to the audience through Marco. This
second-hand retailing of incidents is a common expedient, often used in plays where races or fights
occurring off-stage are told of by one who is
visible to the audience. It is a step beyond the
Messenger in Greek drama, who tells what has
happened rather than, as a present spectator,
what is actually happening at the time. The latter method is more vivid, and is very convenient,
as well as stimulating to the dramatic imagination
of the audience. Note further that after the
crowd is admitted, the tension is still maintained,
as Guido sends the populace home preparatory to
his questioning of Vanna. Then comes the obligatory scene, full of surprises, full of the subtle
touches of the interplay of character upon character, ever tense and throbbing with excitement.
Then comes the scene between Vanna and her husband alone—this is still in the obligatory scene.
Guido still persists in his wilful belief that his wife
is "guilty." The action rises to the point where
Guido condemns Prinzivalle to prison; Monna
Vanna sees the futility of endeavoring to per-
suade her husband that she "is untouched," lies

and declares that "he [Prinzivalle] belongs to
her," begging that she also be incarcerated. The
action has taken another turn, with no fall in interest, but rather a tightening of the strings of
tension; the outcome becomes more and more prob-
lematical. But when (p. 276) Vanna tells Marco,
"Father, he is mine; you shall answer for him.
. . . (She looks fixedly at him.) You understand," the play is over. Guido the blind, utterly
incapable of believing in the virtue that is not that
dictated by convention, in woman's highest virtue,
has lost his wife because of his smallness of soul;
she has gone to one who is more fitted to love and
understand her. "Yes," she says, "it has been a
bad dream . . . but the beautiful one will begin
again. The beautiful one will begin——"

THE BLUE BIRD

A fairy play in six acts. First published 1908.
Translated by Alexander Teixeira de Mattos.

If "The Blue Bird" is not Maeterlinck's greatest play it is undeniably his best known, mainly by
reason of the more or less adequate presentations
on our stage. But there is a great deal—most,
in fact—that is lost through the best of productions, which can only be obtained by careful reading and study of the text. . . . There is so much
in the play, and it may be regarded from so many

angles of vision, that it is difficult not to find something beautiful in the most cursory reading.   It
is a play for children only in that its picturesque
externals are attractive; it is actually an allegor-
ical and symbolical drama, full of philosophical
questionings and high reasoning.   It asks eternal
questions: Whence do we come?   Whither are we
going?   What is death?   What is happiness?
The answer may be somewhat vague, but the questions are squarely put.   The answer may be that
unselfish love, or sacrifice, is true happiness; it may
be that the poet is not quite sure himself, but the
question is all-important.

1. Maeterlinck is a symbolist; * he is a writer
who expresses thoughts in the form of concrete
images, because he believes that in no other way
could these thoughts be so well expressed.   In
some cases it may be necessary to have the key to
the symbol—as in a great deal of the work of
Blake, Mallarmé, and Yeats—but the best symbolism is of the obvious sort.   In " The Blue
Bird," the bird is Happiness personified:† the Dog
is man's friend, the Cat his enemy, and so on.
This symbolism is explained in the two essays referred to in the footnote below; there is no need

* See Arthur Symons, " The Symbolist Movement in Literature " (Heinemann, 1900).

† Henry Rose, in his " Maeterlinck's Symbolism " (Dodd,
Mead, 1911), declares that the " Blue Bird " is the symbol
of " celestial truth."   See also *Poet-Lore*, vol. xxii, No. 6.

to identify the other characters here, the important point is to consider whether the author has
chosen his best, his only medium. Try to imagine
the wandering of Tyltyl and Mytyl incorporated
in a verse drama of conventional structure, or in
a realistic drama—like one of Ibsen's;—treat the
subject in any other way than that which the poet
has chosen to treat it; what would the play lose?

Compare the use of symbolism in " The Blue
Bird " with that of Rostand's " Chantecler "; how
close is the connection between the Cat and the
Blackbird, the Dog and Patou?

2. The exposition is remarkable. The few lines
on the first page (p. 15) make clear the situation,
the time, and give something of the character of
the children.

Tyltyl

Mytyl?

Mytyl

Tyltyl?

Tyltyl

Are you asleep?

Mytyl

Are you?

Tyltyl

No; how can I be asleep when I'm talking to you?

We have already the masculine and rather patronizing attitude of the boy.

Mytyl

Say, is this Christmas Day?

Tyltyl

Not yet; not till to-morrow. But Father Christmas won't bring us anything this year.

Mytyl

Why not?

Tyltyl

I heard mummy say that she couldn't go to town to tell him.—But he will come next year——

Mytyl

Is next year far off?

The time is Christmas Eve, the family is poor, but "in no way poverty-stricken," for the children get Christmas presents every other year. A little later, Mytyl and Tyltyl "get up, run to one of the windows, climb on the stool, and throw back the shutters." And again Tyltyl asserts his superiority. "We can see everything!" he says, but Mytyl, "who can hardly find room on the stool," replies, "I can't." Still farther on (p. 19), we seem to get an indication of the theme of the play.

Mytyl

What are those people doing who are making such a noise?

Tyltyl

They're the musicians.

Mytyl

Arc they angry?

Tyltyl

No; but it's hard work.

Here are people then seeking happiness through the hard work of others. Turn now to the end of the play: happiness is about us, the author demonstrates, and we do not have to " work hard " for it.

With what you have learned of the methods and ends of exposition, trace carefully that of " The Blue Bird," differentiating atmosphere, the story of the past, character, and preparation. Where does the exposition stop and the action proper begin?

3. In nearly every play so far studied there has been a logically developed story with a plot that moved, or " marched." Is there such in " The Blue Bird? " Does the interest lie in the story, in the external events? If so, does each act develop out of the preceding? What is the unity of the play?

D'ANNUNZIO

Gabriele D'Annunzio was born in 1863 at Pescara in the Abruzzi, Italy. He showed an early predilection for poetry, and while at school he published his first verses, at the age of sixteen. After a short schooling in Tuscany, he went to Rome and directed his energies to the writing of poetry and short stories. After the breaking up of the circle to which the young poet belonged, he became a journalist, and published in the *Tribuna* some of his best work. His first novel, " Il Piacere," appeared in 1889; this was followed by other novels—" L'Innocente " and " Giovanni Episcopo "—and later by " Il Trionfo della Morte " and " Il Fuoco," all of which spread his fame abroad. The plays date from the late 'nineties, the " Dream of a Spring Morning " appearing in 1897. With Sarah Bernhardt's production of " The Dead City," D'Annunzio's power as a dramatist began to be universally recognized—a " decadent " to be sure, yet a powerful one. He has recently made Paris his home, and his three latest plays have been written in French, and produced by French actors in Paris.

D'Annunzio is recognized as the greatest force in modern Italian literature; in the fields of lyrical poetry, prose fiction, and the drama, he has not yet been surpassed by his own countrymen. Fogazzaro

was as great a novelist, but his plays are of little
importance; Giacosa's novels are conceded to be inferior to his plays, while the latter lack that lyric
power which in D'Annunzio is everywhere manifest.
D'Annunzio is the perfect type of esthete, his is the
religion of beauty: what is beautiful is good. In
" Gioconda " (Act I, Scene 3) Cosimo Dalbo says
". . . so much sorrow shall not have been suffered in
vain, so much evil shall not have been useless, if one
thing so beautiful remains over, to be added to the
ornament of life." And Lucio Settala replies, " It is
true. I sometimes think of the fate of one whose ship
and all that was in it went down in a storm. On a day
as calm as this, he took a boat and a net, and he returned to the place of the shipwreck, hoping to draw
something out of the depths. And, after much labor,
he drew on shore a statue. And the statue was so
beautiful that he wept for joy to see it again; and he
sat down on the sea-shore to gaze upon it, and was
content with that gain, and would seek nothing more:
. . . I forgot the rest! "—The man on the sea-shore
is D'Annunzio himself; he sees what is beautiful, in
character, in setting, in style. We may not agree
with him, but we are forced to admit that his aspirations are for what is best in sheer poetic beauty. His
choice of subject is often " unpleasant "; in the
" Dead City " it is incest, and in the " Dream of an
Autumn Sunset " and " The Ship " the themes are no
less revolting. It is for this reason that D'Annunzio
is called " decadent "; he is undoubtedly morbid, abnormal, and at times almost hysterical, but the fine

feeling for the perfection of style, the skilful treatment of those phases of life which he has chosen to depict, are ample recompense for any incidental or even inherent unpleasantness in subject.

PLAYS

The Dream of a Spring Morning (1897).

The Dream of an Autumn Sunset (1898).

La Gioconda (1899).

> Produced in Italian in New York by Duse 1902; given a few performances in French by Mme. Yorska 1914.

The Dead City (1898).

> Produced in New York by Duse 1902.

Glory (1899).

Francesca da Rimini (1901).

> Produced in New York by Duse 1902.

The Daughter of Jorio (1904).

Greater than Love (1907).

The Ship (1908).

Fedra (1909).

The Light Under the Bushel (1909).

The Martyrdom of St. Sebastian (1912).

Pisanella, or the Perfumed Death (1913).

The Honeysuckle (1914).

" The Dream of a Spring Morning " is translated by Anna Schenck (*Poet-Lore*, 1902); " The Dream of an Autumn Sunset " by Anna Schenck (*Poet-Lore*, 1904); " La Gioconda " by Arthur Symons (Russell, 1902); " The Dead City " by G. Mantellini (Laird,

Chicago, 1902), and by Arthur Symons (Heinemann,
1902); "Francesca da Rimini" by Arthur Symons
(Stokes, 1902); "The Daughter of Jorio" by Char-
lotte Porter, Pietro Isola, and Alice Henry (Little,
Brown, 1907; also *Poet-Lore,* 1911); "The Ship"
(*Poet-Lore,* 1909).

REFERENCES: James Huneker, "Iconoclasts";
Ashley Dukes, "Modern Dramatists"; Addison Mc-
Leod, "Plays and Players of Modern Italy" (Ser-
gel, 1912); W. L. Courtney, "The Development of
Maurice Maeterlinck, and Other Sketches of Foreign
Writers" (Grant Richards, 1904); Arthur Symons,
"Studies in Prose and Verse" (Heinemann, 1904);
Oscar Heermann, "Living Dramatists" (Brentano,
1905).—*Magazines: Poet-Lore,* vol. xix, Nos. 1 and 2;
Bookman, vol. iii (p. 18); *Critic,* vol. xlvii (p. 27),
and vol. xlv (p. 137), and vol. xli (p. 103); *Dial,* vol.
xxxiv (p. 7); *Fortnightly,* vol. lxxiv (p. 391). See
also "Modern Drama and Opera: A Reading List"
(Boston Book Co., 1911) for bibliography, as well as
the introductions to the translations of "The Dead
City" and "The Daughter of Jorio."

GIOCONDA

A tragedy in four acts. First published 1899. Translated by Arthur Symons.

1. The first act is an admirable piece of construction: clear-cut and natural in exposition;
moving, and unified. Character is exposed, the
past unfolded, almost before the reader is aware

that he is learning anything; and the play has
begun in earnest by the time the curtain falls.

A first act should never leave one in doubt as to
what sort of play he is seeing; it should let him
know whether he is to see comedy or tragedy,
farce or melodrama. Such indications are nearly
always made early in the course of the action or
exposition of the first act. In " Gioconda," Silvia
Settala's words (p. 5) foreshadow the serious turn
affairs will later take: " Then, do you know, a
breath passed, a vapor, a mere nothing, and cast
down everything, and the anxiety came back, and
the dread, and the tremor! " These lines and the
spirit in which they are spoken, forebode evil; the
more so as everything is so apparently calm for the
remainder of the act. We feel instinctively that
this is the calm before the tempest. Were the
play to turn out well, complications would have
immediately set in, and a happy event would be
foreshadowed; instead, all is outward happiness,
which we may take as a foreshadowing of evil.—
This indication is necessary, as the audience must
know where to place its sympathies, and in what
frame of mind to listen to the play; otherwise, it
might be unsettled, bewildered.

2. Although the first act is a definite unit of
action in itself, it leaves us a little curious to know
the precise direction that the action will take; a
trained reader or listener will vaguely anticipate a

struggle between Silvia and the opposing forces: in this case, the object of Lucio's former love. The second act should reveal unmistakably this struggle, let us know the contending parties, and show us at least the alternative possibilities and probable direction of the plot. As we are told (in the original edition, not the translation) that the play is a tragedy, it is not difficult to surmise that the peaceful relations as seen in the first act between Silvia and Lucio will be broken off in tragic fashion—just how, the next three acts will show.

The second act opens with a note of warning. Gioconda, the model, is heard from, and Lucio's " No, no, no," preceded by the stage direction " (With a shudder of dread) " (p. 44), leaves little room for speculation as to the direction the story will take: Lucio will return to his mistress. With great rapidity the struggle becomes more clearly defined. The conversation between Lucio and Cosimo, culminating in the former's long speech (pp. 54-59), begins to make us aware of the inevitability of Lucio's relapse, that Gioconda is still his " ideal." Lucio's love for her is the result of his personality, it is deeply imbedded in his soul; because of this fatal attraction, and in spite of his " good " resolutions, Lucio will bring suffering upon himself, his wife, and family.—A further element in the struggle is introduced as Silvia (p. 70) resolves to meet Gioconda and try to get the key of Lucio's studio from her; the obligatory scene is anticipated, the struggle in its culmination, the climax. The next act must be taken up with the contest.

3. The studio, where else? Note that Gioconda is not introduced at once; the scene must begin at low tension and work up to a big " situation." Silvia states the case at once (p. 93) to her rival, " One of us two is the intruder. Which? "—and the scene begins. Silvia argues eloquently, passionately, but Gioconda is confident in her strength, until Silvia tells her to go; that precipitates the actual struggle, which ends in the attempted destruction of the statue, and the " lacerating cry from Silvia, torn by agony from her very vitals " (p. 109). This is the climax. A short staccato scene, with Lucio and Francesco, ends the act. Again the outcome is uncertain.

4. The struggle is over; between the third and fourth acts Lucio has succumbed to his old love and gone away with Gioconda. D'Annunzio's description of Silvia (p. 113) tells the story: " Silvia Settala appears on the threshold, from the inner room; she pauses; takes several steps towards the window; looks into the distance, looks about her with infinitely sad eyes." And we know at once what has happened. " Silvia may make her home a haven of peace; she may tend and nurse her husband when the other woman drives him to attempt

self-destruction; she may fondle him with caresses
and words of love as beautiful as ever flowed from
woman's lips; she may lie for his sake, she may
sacrifice her beautiful hands to save his statue
from the violence of her rival—she may do all this
and more, yet the other conquers all along the line,
for she is the mate of his being, his body, his ego,
and Silvia's love is but the placid affection which
neither satisfies nor inspires the high-strung, in-
satiable soul of the creative artist." *

This last act is in many ways an ideal one.
First, it carries the story to a logical conclusion;
second, it sustains the interest up to the end;
third, it gradually brings us back to the level
whence it began; and finally, it contains that gentle
chastening or cleansing element—in this case, the
tragedy and sweetness of mother-love, combined
with sympathetic care—that gives to true tragedy
a lasting quality and brings it close to what is best
in life. The scene that closes the play is terrible,
but its terror inspires the further element of pity,
not revulsion: this is true tragic beauty.

Compare the rather unemphatic ending of "Gioconda" with the tense and decidedly emphatic last
act of Echegaray's "Madman or Saint" (p. 224,
present volume).

* J. T. Grein, in "Premières of the Year" (John Mac-
queen, London, 1900).

GIACOSA

Giuseppe Giacosa * was born at Colleretto Parella, Italy, in 1847. After studying for the Law in Turin, he began at once the career of a man of letters; this was early in the 'seventies. He "resided during the first part of his literary career in Turin and later at Milan. He came to America in 1891." . . . During the last years of his life and up to the time of his death he was director of the magazine *La Lettura*. He died in the town where he was born in 1906.

It is impossible to make an extensive study of the modern Italian drama in English, as the works of only three or four authors are translated, and of these a number of D'Annunzio's are still untranslated, and all but two of Giacosa's. But in spite of French influence—which has done much to harm, and somewhat to benefit, the Italian drama—there are a number of original and interesting playwrights: † Roberto Bracco,‡ E. A. Butti, Giannino Antona-Traversé, Sem

* For the material contained in most of this sketch of Giacosa, I am indebted to Stanley Astrado Smith, whose article on Giacosa appeared in *The Drama,* May, 1913.

† Jean Dornis has written (in French) a very complete work on the contemporary Italian drama, "Le Théâtre Italien d'aujourd'hui" (Calmann-Lévy, Paris).

‡ *Poet-Lore* contains translations of "Phantasms" and "The Hidden Spring" (1908 and 1907).

Benelli, Marco Praga, and Gerolamo Rovetta, are
among this number.* But, taking into account the
sum-total of their dramatic work, D'Annunzio and Giacosa are undoubtedly the most important exponents of
the modern Italian drama. Giacosa it was who, more
than any other, infused a true Italian element into his
best plays; he did much to free the stage of his country
from French adaptations and pseudo-French "triangle" plays. "As the Leaves" was rightfully
hailed by the Italian press as epoch-making, and to its
influence many serious and original works may be
traced.

PLAYS

A GAME OF CHESS (1872).

AN OLD STORY (1872).

TO A DOG THAT LICKS ASHES DO NOT GIVE
FLOUR † (1872).

DON'T SAY FLOUR UNLESS YOU HAVE IT IN THE
SACK † (1872).

BANK AFFAIRS (1873).

THE SONS OF THE MARQUIS ARTURO (1874).

SAD DOUBTS (1874).

GALLANT INTRIGUES (1874).

THE TRIUMPH OF LOVE (1875).

NOCTURNAL SURPRISES (1875).

A CANDIDATE (1875).

TERESA (1875).

MOUNTAIN SHOWERS (1876).

* See Addison McLeod, "Plays and Players of Modern
Italy" (Sergel, 1912).

† Common Italian proverbs.

The Brothers-at-Arms (1877).

The Red Count (1880).

Luise (1881).

The Thread (1883).

The Siren (1883).

A Surrender to Discretion (1885).

The Honorable Ercole Mallardi (1885).

Sad Loves (1888).

The Belated Repentance (1888).

The Lady of Challont (1891).

Produced in New York by Mme. Bernhardt 1891.

The Rights of the Soul (1894).

As the Leaves (1900). Produced by Donald Robertson, Chicago 1908.

The Stronger (1904). Produced by the Drama Players, Chicago 1911.

Besides the above are the libretti (in collaboration with Luigi Illica) for " La Bohème " (1896), " Tosca " (1899), and " Madame Butterfly " (1903); together with numerous other one-act plays.

Translations of " As the Leaves " and " The Stronger " are published in *The Drama* (February, 1911, and May, 1913). " The Stronger," " Like Falling Leaves," and " Sacred Ground " (" The Rights of the Soul ") are translated by Edith and Allan Updegraff (Kennerley, 1913). An adaptation of " A Game of Chess " by Barrett H. Clark is published by Samuel French (1914).

References: Stanley Astrado Smith (*The Drama,* May, 1913); Addison McLeod, " Plays and Players of Modern Italy " (Sergel, 1912).

AS THE LEAVES

A comedy in four acts. First published 1900. Translation in *The Drama,* and by E. and A. Updegraff.

1. " As the Leaves " may well be considered one of the finest examples of the modern social comedy. Its truth to life, its strong yet sympathetic treatment of phases of life that are common to most of humanity, and its mastery of construction—all combine to " take us out of ourselves," to create the illusion that we are participating in an actual family struggle. Starting at a level with life, the action gradually mounts from crisis to crisis, and finally falls back to life again, leaving us with a sense of having experienced something exhilarating, ennobling, helpful.

In studying the play, notice the natural and extremely skilful manner in which incident follows incident, how one situation grows out of the preceding, and how the entire work springs into existence as life itself, and not as if conjured into being at the will of even a great craftsman. The skill of the dramatist is hardly noticed, so admirably has he covered his footmarks.

2. The play is so well constructed, that a too detailed analysis of its component parts might prevent our enjoying it as a whole, for a *first reading,* however. Read it therefore in the same spirit as you would go to the theater: for the pure en-

joyment of the story, and afterwards analyze it and inquire into the methods employed to give it its consistency and charm.

A word as to the characterization. As is right, no character is essentially bad or good, and in his treatment Giacosa's warm-hearted sympathy and interest in humanity are keenly felt. We feel sorry for Tommy and Giulia, as well as for Rosani and Nennele; and if Tommy is snobbish, Nennele is stubborn, if Giulia is frivolous, Giovanni is at times weak; while even the delightful Massimo has a too pronounced tendency to preach.

The situation, too, is an admirable one—this reversal of the family fortunes—and serves well to bring out the essential characteristics of each of the persons involved. Since action is one of the essentials of a good play, each of these persons must do something, and since all are acting under unusual stress, we see new sides and a further development of their characters. Again, Giacosa shows his skill; he knew precisely where to begin his play.

3. Every play—and every act in every play—ought to advance (1) either the story or (2) the development of the characters. As a section of life cannot be lived or observed without leaving us better or worse, so a play or an act of a play affects us, for better or for worse. The end should be either higher or lower than the beginning; we

must be either elevated or degraded. Much depends upon the dramatist for this effect—some on the auditor. In " As the Leaves " the end of each act leaves one on a higher level than the beginning: he knows more of the motives of the characters, of their doings and their thoughts, than at the beginning. The first act, for example, shows us the family preparing to go away; we know nothing of them. Before the end of the act, the essential traits of Tommy, Nennele, Giulia, and, to a certain extent, of Rosani, are clearly outlined.

Trace this development in the case of each of the succeeding acts.

4. The last act is short.—Why is this? First, there is little material, and the author has a wholesome aversion to " stringing out " his last act. Second, a dramatic reason: a short scene, if it have movement and suspense, is very effective on the stage. Nennele, discouraged at the apparent loss of Massimo, at the weakness of Tommy and her step-mother, has determined to take her own life. Her suicide would have been too tragical an outcome, especially as the father is not so weak as Nennele thought him, and as Massimo " did understand," and did come back to her.—Nor is the " happy " ending a concession to the audience; in this case, it is almost as inevitable as are the respective suicides in " Mid-Channel " or " Hedda Gabler." After Tommy and Giulia drift and fall

away " as the leaves," something definite is required to end the play: Aristotle's rule is applicable to all art forms, for there must be a beginning, a middle, and an end.   A slice of life, in
order to be a work of art, must be secure at each
end, so to speak, and not be left suspended in
mid-air.

ECHEGARAY

José Echegaray, the chief exponent of the modern Spanish drama, was born in Madrid in 1832. Ever an apt pupil, at an early age he showed a distinct inclination for mathematics and the exact sciences; although he was attracted to the study of science, he showed a great liking for literature and the theater, and in later years he read widely in the drama of the modern nations of Europe. He was graduated in 1853 from the Escuela de Caminos, with high honors, and became a tutor of mathematics. Not long afterward, he was made a professor of that subject in the school from which he graduated. From that time on, his interests widened; he studied Political Economy, Philosophy, Geology, and Politics. Besides these pursuits, he engaged in those of Engineering and Physics, and was recognized as an authority. At the age of thirty-two he wrote a play, but laid it aside, deeming it unworthy; but his interest in drama was steadily increasing. He was appointed Minister for the Colonies, under the government following the Revolution of 1868, and his political duties prevented further development of his dramatic genius. Five years later he was proscribed, forced to leave the country, and go to France, where he wrote his first play that was produced, "El Libro Talonario." On his return to Spain in 1874, it was presented, but did not attract great attention. His first success was "En el Puño la Espada" (1875), and was followed by a long series of tragedies, comedies, and thesis plays.

"Spaniards declare that for more than 200 years their drama has not brought forth a serious rival to this man. And there can hardly be a doubt that, in any selection of names of the great dramatists Lope de Vega and Calderon de la Barca will find the place nearest to themselves occupied by José Echegaray." *

The Spanish drama of to-day is of more importance than is commonly thought.† Echegaray and Galdós, both living, and the latter still writing, are of world-wide repute, and occupy a high position among contemporary dramatists, while there are half a dozen other Spaniards—as yet untranslated—who are producing work of great originality; Jacinto Benavente, Angel Guimera, Sierra, and Serafin and his brother Joaquin Quintero, are among these. Their work is as a whole witty, refined, and carefully finished. It is just, however, that only the two principal writers should be here considered; of the two Echegaray, in the realm of the drama, is the greater.

* See Introduction to Graham's translation of "The Son of Don Juan" (Roberts Bros., Boston, 1895).

† Miss Elizabeth Wallace, author of the article (*Atlantic Monthly,* vol. cii, p. 357) on "The Spanish Drama of To-day," has kindly supplied me with most of the above information.

PLAYS

THE CHECK BOOK (1874).

THE WIFE OF THE AVENGER (1874).

THE GREAT GALEOTTO (1874).

    Produced in New York in 1900, in German by
Kainz 1891. In 1909 Mr. Faversham and Miss
Julie Opp produced a very free version entitled
" The World and His Wife."

THE LAST NIGHT (1875).

AT THE HILT OF THE SWORD (1875).

THE BEGINNING AND THE END (1876).

MADMAN OR SAINT (1877). Robertson, Chicago 1908.

WHAT CANNOT BE TOLD (1877).

BEFORE THE PILLAR AND THE CROSS (1878).

IN PURSUIT OF AN IDEAL (1878).

SOMETIMES BELOW (1878).

IN THE BOSOM OF DEATH (1879).

SHORELESS SEA (1879).

DEATH ON THE LIPS (1880).

HAROLD THE NORMAN (1881).

THE TWO CURIOSITY MONGERS (1882).

CONFLICT BETWEEN TWO DUTIES (1882).

A MIRACLE IN EGYPT (1883).

IN SUPPOSING EVIL. WILL YOU GUESS? (1884).

THE PEST OF OTRANTO (1884).

HAPPY LIFE, SAD DEATH (1885).

LYSANDER THE BANDIT (1886).

EVIL RACE (1886).

TWO FANATICISMS (1887).

REALITY AND DELIRIUM (1887).

THE SON OF STEEL AND THE SON OF FLESH (1888).

The Sublime in the Commonplace (1888).

Everlasting Source of Troubles (1889).

The Extremists (1889).

Ever Ridiculous (1890).

The Embryo Critic (1891).

Comedy Without Dénouement (1891).

The Son of Don Juan (1892).

Sic vos, non vobis, or The Last Alms (1892).

Mariana (1892).

    Produced in New York by Mrs. Patrick Campbell 1902.

The Power of Impotence (1893).

At the Sea-Shore (1893).

The Enraged Lady (1894).

Try Who Washes (1895).

The Stigmata (1895).

Wild Love (1896).

Calumny as a Chastisement (1897).

The Doubt (1898).

The Man in Black (1898).

The Silence of Death (1898).

The Madman Divine (1900).

Accursed Heritages (1902).

The Steps of a Throne (1903).

The Unstable One (1903).

Letting Oneself Be Dragged Along (1905).

A number of one-act plays, adaptations, translations, operas, etc., have been omitted from the above list. For a complete list see Henri de Curzon, " Le Théâtre de José Echegaray " (Librairie Fischbacher, Paris, 1912).

"Madman or Saint" is translated by Ruth Lansing (*Poet-Lore,* 1912), by Hannah Lynch as "Folly or Saintliness" (Lane, London, 1895); "The Great Galeoto" by Hannah Lynch, in the same volume, as "Folly or Saintliness," and later separately (Doubleday) and in an adaptation, "The World and His Wife," by C. F. Nirdlinger (Kennerley, 1908); "The Son of Don Juan," by James Stewart (Roberts Bros., Boston, 1895); "Mariana" by the same (Roberts Bros., 1895), and by Fredico Sarda and Carlos D. S. Wuppermann (Moods Publishing Co., New York, 1909); "The Man in Black" by Ellen Watson (*Universal Anthology,* vol. xxvii); and "The Madman Divine" by Elizabeth Howard West (*Poet-Lore,* 1908).

REFERENCES: The introductions to the Lynch and Stewart translations give much material; for special articles see *Atlantic,* vol. cii (p. 357); *Poet-Lore,* vol. xii (p. 405), vol. xx (p. 218); *Contemporary Review,* vol. lxiv (p. 576); *Review of Reviews,* vol. xxxi (p. 613). For individual criticisms see Bernard Shaw's "Dramatic Opinions and Essays" (Brentano, 1907), and C. F. Nirdlinger, "Masks and Mummers" (De Witt Publishing House, New York, 1899).

MADMAN OR SAINT

A drama in three acts. First published 1877. Translations by Ruth Lansing and Hannah Lynch.

1. In order to understand much in the Spanish drama, some knowledge of Spanish traditions of

chivalry, family and personal honor, is necessary. This is especially true of Spain's greatest and most representative dramatist, Calderon (1600-1681); honor may be said to be the
principal character in many of Spain's greatest
plays, of all ages. In Calderon's " Physician of
His Own Honor" (1633) "a lover has wandered
about in her [the heroine's] vicinity—she must
die." Echegaray, in " Madman or Saint," treats
the question from the standpoint of honor in relation to the family name. Unless the reader
understands that this matter of honor is little
short of an obsession with the Spaniards, he can
have little sympathy with their drama.

2. " Madman or Saint " illustrates as few other
plays * do the principle of suspense. From the
end of the first act to the very end of the last, the
action rises steadily; never until the final curtain
falls does Don Lorenzo's fate become a certainty.
Let us examine into the means employed to attain
this end.

Lorenzo tells the Duchess (p. 182, *Poet-Lore*
translation) " this marriage is impossible "; the
struggle begins, and the outcome is very prob-
lematical. The contending parties are known at
once: Lorenzo is on one side, and in all probability
Angela, Inez, Edward, and Thomas are against

* Brieux's "La Robe Rouge" (The Red Robe) is, however, one of these.

him. Early in the second act (p. 183) Edward foreshadows the outcome, in his words: " Lorenzo shall give in if we have to put a gag and strait-jacket on him." Then (same page) the struggle has begun to be defined, as Edward says, " We must either take Mr. Lorenzo as a joke or shut him up in an asylum." The question arises, Is Lorenzo a madman or is he a saint? A little later (p. 184) the Duchess heightens the interest by doubting Lorenzo's motives, as she declares that " to be the grandchild of a humble nurse, an accomplice in having usurped a social position, is the future of that poor girl, if what Mr. Lorenzo says is so." Again, Edward (p. 187) brings the matter to a clearer issue: . . . "everything depends on Mr. Lorenzo." Then follow a series of dialogues between Lorenzo and his opponents—in the dramatic sense: those who want something in direct opposition to his wishes. Lorenzo's sense of honor and his love for his daughter and wife are the real contending forces; he himself cares little for the external forces—Edward, the Duchess, and Thomas. Through all these scenes the struggle becomes sharper, the issues stand out more plainly. For a moment (p. 192) Lorenzo seems to waver (" What is truth? What is false-hood? ") Then (p. 193) his love for Inez and Angela is almost too much for him: " But you, beloved women, you, my Inez, why must you go before me, marking with your tears the road my feet must stain with blood? I alone, so be it, but not you. My God, help me, for the light of my conscience is dying down, my will is failing, despair is taking possession of my mind." The entrance of Jane takes his mind away from his doubts, and he regains strength to carry out his resolution. We have already seen that it is unwise to keep a secret from the audience; no further justification of the principle can be seen than that which is at hand. Knowing Lorenzo's determination to give up his family name, Jane destroys the only proof (p. 196) upon which Lorenzo can base his assertion that his is not the name which rightfully belongs to him. The stage direction reads: " Throws letter into the fire and bends down to watch it burn." The audience therefore, as Jane soon dies, is the only party let into this secret, and assumes its " God-like attitude," awaiting the outcome; the strings draw tighter round Lorenzo, and his ultimate hope, he sees, will be the justification of his actions through the proof of the letter. His opponents will soon resort to desperate methods. The tension therefore grows with every scene, as the outcome becomes more and more uncertain. If the destruction of the letter and the substitution of the blank were unknown to every one, including, and above all, the audience, the suspense would be greatly lessened;

we, as interested spectators of the misfortunes and struggles of humanity should have lost the "looking-forwardness," as it were, given by a foreknowledge of the catastrophe. If Lorenzo has the proof, or if he thinks he has it, there is little doubt that he will adduce it at the necessary moment, and all will be well; but if we know he does not have it, another element of suspense is added, and the tension is therefore much greater. Again, we are forced to ask, What will happen? Jane's deathbed denial of the story furthers the case against Lorenzo, who is momentarily defeated. He is sure, though, because he has the proof, which he will bring forth when the time is ripe. Lorenzo's opponents, seeing him bent on the fulfilment of his determination, resolve that they will conquer, and Thomas brings in the alienist and his assistants; Lorenzo must be taken away if he is mad— and it seems that such is the case: seems, that is, to all but the audience. Still further suspense is gained (p. 204) as Lorenzo makes sure that his letter is in its place. From this point on the letter becomes the center of interest, and the climax, or crux, of the entire play is plainly in view: Lorenzo is either sane, and in consequence, a saint (but he must give ample proof of his sanity), or else (lacking proof of this) he is mad. Everything depends on the proof, and the proof is the letter. Now the audience knows the letter is gone, and wants to see how Lorenzo will behave when he learns this, and how his family and friends will behave toward him. The tension is greater than ever before. Consider, now, how much of this emotional stress would have been lost had we known nothing of the destruction of the letter; at the end of the play we should have experienced a shock of surprise, that is all; now, every moment, we are feeling emotions that are fundamental in the drama, emotions for which we pay and which we wish to have, and would be ill-content without: curiosity and suspense.

Note (p. 215) how a last touch is added to the pathos of Lorenzo's position, in his words, " I almost pity the traitors. The security of my triumph sustains me." Then (p. 217) comes the highest point in the play (bottom of p. 217, and top of following page); this is the veritable climax. The *dénouement* is meteoric, and occupies only two pages. Lorenzo is conquered by force of circumstances, and is taken away as a madman; this is the catastrophe.

3. Compare this play, for subject-matter and treatment, with Ibsen's " An Enemy of the People." Contrast the ending of each, and the conclusions reached.

THE GREAT GALEOTTO

A play in three acts and a prologue. First published
1874. Translated by Hannah Lynch.

" The Great Galeotto " is one of the finest examples
of the thesis play. The thesis is made clear in the
Prologue and during the course of the play proper
is never lost sight of, yet never are the situations or
the characters in any way strained to the detriment
of the truth, or the verisimilitude of the story.
Theme and plot go hand in hand, and are so admirably welded that if either were developed more
than it is, the play would suffer as an artistic unit.
The skill with which the thesis is handled is the more
remarkable when we consider that Echegaray had very
little experience at the time he was writing. Augier
and Dumas fils, the originators of the modern thesis
play, were still at work, and were both to write some
of their most characteristic pieces, while Ibsen had
hardly begun his social plays.

1. Compare the Prologue of the " Great
Galeotto " with that of Andreyeff's " Anathema "
and Alexandre Bisson's " Madame X " (La
Femme X).* Of what use is the introductory act?
Why does not the author either call it the first act
or, omitting it entirely, introduce the material

* Untranslated. The play has been produced in the United
States, notably by Sarah Bernhardt and Dorothy Donnelly.

into the exposition of his next (and consequently first) act?

2. For psychological and artistic reasons, we are now aware, a dramatist must vary his scenes. Study Echegaray's methods in the second act.

3. In the Nirdlinger version ("The World and His Wife," published by Kennerley), new characters are introduced, and the time of the play has been changed. Compare the original with this stage version. Which is the better, and why?

4. At the time when this play was written, the soliloquy and aside had not gone out of style; yet how does Echegaray handle these? Had Pinero, for instance, been writing the play, in what way could he have modified the dialogue so as to do away with these "worn-out conventions"?

5. Which is structurally the better play, "The Great Galeotto" or "Madman or Saint"? Consider the works as stories; which is the more effectively presented? Which, on the stage (so far as you are able to visualize them), would be more interesting to the average audience?

6. Echegaray's theme is universal: the tongue of more or less innocent gossip does incomparable harm. In her little one-act comedy "Spreading the News" (Maunsel, Dublin), Lady Gregory treats much the same theme, but from its comic side. In what other respects are the plays similar?

7. Does the author consider the Prologue as

his first act? That is, does he include in it all the exposition proper, and build from it to the development and climax? See Question 1, present discussion.

8. If some characters had of necessity to be eliminated from the play, which would go first, with the least injury to the whole? Has Echegaray practised that economy in the number of characters which is so essential to the drama?

GALDOS

Benito Perez Galdós, like Echegaray, is one of Spain's foremost writers; though better known as a novelist—" Marianela " and " Doña Perfecta " are celebrated; yet his plays have nevertheless placed him in the front rank of dramatists. He was born in the Canary Islands, at Las Palmas, in 1845. At an early age he went to Madrid, with the intention of studying law, but finding this work unsuited to his taste, turned to journalism. He soon began writing fiction, and wrote a series of romances—National Episodes—that, with a further and subsequent series, have made his name known throughout his own country and Europe.* He did not turn to drama seriously until late in his career—the plays date from the early 'nineties to 1905.

Galdós's plays are many of them dramatizations of

* " In fecundity and in the power of creating characters, Perez-Galdós vies with Balzac. Parallel with his immense achievement in historical fiction, Perez-Galdós published a collection of romances dealing with contemporary life, its social problems and religious difficulties. Of these the best-known, and perhaps the best, are ' Doña Perfecta ' (1876), ' Gloria ' (1877), ' La Familia Leon Roch ' (1878), ' Marianela ' (1878), ' Fortunata y Jacinta ' (1887), and ' Angel Guerra ' (1891)." From article Perez-Galdós, Benito; Encyclopedia Britannica, 11th ed., vol. xxi, pp. 139-40.

his own novels, done by himself; some of them suffer because of this process, but those belonging to his later period arc perhaps better, because the author knows better how to combine his knowledge of the drama with that of fiction, thereby giving his plays breadth and character.

As throughout all Spanish literature, we find in the plays of this writer an insistence on the "Honor" theme; in "The Grandfather" it is of great importance. In fact, the play is built upon it. The novel ending of the play is something of a modern innovation. This will be considered in our more detailed study.

PLAYS

REALITY (1892).
MAD FOR THE SAKE OF THE FAMILY (1893).
THE DUCHESS OF ST. QUENTIN (1894).
THE CONDEMNED (1894).
WILL (1895).
DONA PERFECTA (1896).
THE WILD BEAST (1896).
ELECTRA (1901).
SOUL AND LIFE (1902).
MARIUCHA (1903).
THE GRANDFATHER (1904).
BARBARA (1905).
LOVE AND SCIENCE (1905).

A translation of "Electra" is published in *The Drama,* May, 1911; and one of "The Grandfather" by Elizabeth Wallace in *Poet-Lore,* 1911.

REFERENCES: *Drama,* May, 1911; *Atlantic,* vol. cii (p. 358); *Era,* vol. x (p. 535); *Critic,* vol. xxxix (p. 213); and vol. xlv (p. 447).

THE GRANDFATHER

A drama in five acts. First published 1904. Translated by Elizabeth Wallace.

1. " The Grandfather," besides being a good acting play, is a psychological study of a revolution in a man's soul. The struggle is clearly defined: it takes place in the mind of the Count. Which shall conquer: the honor of a noble lineage, or love for his granddaughter, independent of her birth? There is a curious similarity of theme in " Silas Marner " and " The Grandfather "; in the novel the consuming passion of the old man is replaced by the love for the child; Galdós's theme may also be stated in the same terms.

Compare further the novel and the play, and notice in what other respects the Spanish and English underlying ideas are akin.

2. This play is not technically " up-to-date "; the soliloquy, used in unnatural ways, is one indication of the fact. The end of the first act (p. 180) is somewhat infelicitous; the Count's outburst seems out of place. The problem before the dramatist was, how to let the audience know that Lucretia was " a monster of wickedness." . . .

Many methods were open to him: conversation, cross-examination of friends—any but the one adopted. To have the Count suddenly burst forth with, "Poor foolish town, she who comes to you is a monster of wickedness; an infamous forger: Do not welcome her; stone her and throw her out," is certainly old-fashioned in the deprecatory sense of the term.

See the end of the first act of Wilde's "Lady Windermere's Fan" for a similar situation, a little better handled.

3. The girls Nell and Dolly form a delightful contrast to the old Count; indeed, they supply the entire dramatic element of variety. Trace this out, and notice how at many of the important crises of each act they balance the other characters. They are furthermore the center of dramatic interest throughout, for the great question as to which is the legitimate heiress to the old family name is always present, and the Count, to whose interest it is to know which is truly his granddaughter, forms the other balancing force.

4. As a review of the principles already taken up, consider the structure, dialogue, and characterization of "The Grandfather," and determine, so far as you are able, what plays of other nations it resembles; whether it is a comedy, farce, melodrama, social play, thesis play, or what, or whether it is a combination of two or more of these.

5. In Echegaray's " Madman or Saint " we considered the principle of suspense. Compare Galdós's treatment of the same principle in this play,
and determine whether Echegaray's or Galdós's
treatment is superior.

BIBLIOGRAPHY

I. General reference works on the drama, its theory, technique, and history:

ARCHER, WILLIAM.

Playmaking, a Manual of Craftsmanship. Small, Maynard, 1912. ($2.00.)

ARCHER, FRANK.

How to Write a Good Play. Samuel French. ($1.75.)

BURTON, RICHARD.

How to See a Play. Macmillan, 1914. ($1.25.)

CAFFIN, CHARLES H. ,

The Appreciation of the Drama. Baker and Taylor, 1908. ($1.50.)

CHENEY, SHELDON.

The New Movement in the Theatre. Kennerley. ($2.00.)

CLARK, BARRETT H.

With a Preface by Brieux Four Plays of the Free Theater. Stewart & Kidd, 1915. ($1.50.)

COURTNEY, W. L.

The Idea of Tragedy. Brentano, 1900.

CRAIG, GORDON.

On the Art of the Theatre. Charles H. Sergel, Chicago, 1912. ($2.00.)

FREYTAG, GUSTAV.

The Technique of the Drama. Scott, Foresman
& Co., 1895. ($1.50).

HAMILTON, CLAYTON.

The Theory of the Theatre. Holt, 1910.
($1.50.)

Studies in Stagecraft. Holt, 1914. ($1.50.)

HENNEQUIN, ALFRED.

The Art of Playwriting. Houghton Mifflin,
1890. ($1.00).

HUNT, ELIZABETH R.

The Play of To-day, Studies in Structure.
Lane, 1913. ($1.50.)

MATTHEWS, BRANDER.

The Development of the Drama. Scribner,
1903. ($1.50.)

A Study of the Drama. Houghton Mifflin, 1910.
($1.50.)

MEREDITH, GEORGE.

An Essay on Comedy, and the Uses of the Comic
Spirit. Scribner, 1897. ($1.00.)

PRICE, WILLIAM T.

The Technique of the Drama. Brentano, 1892.
($1.50.)

Analysis of Play Construction and Dramatic
Principles. W. T. Price, 1908. ($5.00.)

THORNDIKE, ASHLEY H.

Tragedy. Houghton Mifflin, 1908. ($1.50.)

VAUGHN, C. E.

Types of Tragic Drama. Macmillan, 1908.
($1.60.)

WOODBRIDGE, ELIZABETH.

The Drama, Its Law and Technique. Allyn and
Bacon, 1898. (80c.)

II. Books on the modern drama and the modern
theater:

ANDREWS, CHARLTON.

The Drama To-day. Lippincott. ($1.50.)

ARCHER, WILLIAM.

About the Theatre. Unwin, London, 1886.

ARCHER, WILLIAM, and GRANVILLE BARKER.

Scheme and Estimates for a National Theatre.
Duffield, 1908. ($3.50.)

CARTER, HUNTLEY.

The New Spirit in Drama and Art. Palmer.

DUKES, ASHLEY.

Modern Dramatists. Sergel, 1912. ($1.50.)

FILON, AUGUSTIN.

The English Stage. Dodd, Mead, 1897.

Modern French Drama. Chapman and Hall,
London, 1898.

GEORGE, W. L.

Dramatic Actualities. Sidgwick & Jackson, 1914.

GOLDMANN, EMMA.

The Social Significance of the Modern Drama.
Badger, 1914. ($1.00.)

HALE, EDWARD EVERETT, JR.

Dramatists of To-day. Holt, 1905.
(Revised 1912. $1.50.)

HELLER, OTTO.

Studies in Modern German Literature. Ginn &
Co., 1905. ($1.50.)

HENDERSON, ARCHIBALD.

European Dramatists. Stewart & Kidd, 1913. ($1.50.)

The Changing Drama. Holt, 1914. ($1.50.)

HOWE, P. P.

The Repertory Theatre. Kennerley, 1911. ($1.00.)

Dramatic Portraits. Kennerley, 1913. ($1.50.)

HUNEKER, JAMES.

Iconoclasts. Scribner, 1905. ($1.50.)

JONES, HENRY ARTHUR.

The Renascence of the English Drama. Macmillan, 1895. ($1.50.)

The Foundations of a National Drama. Doran, 1913. ($2.50.)

MACKAYE, PERCY.

The Playhouse and the Play. Macmillan, 1909.

The Civic Theatre. Kennerley, 1912. ($1.25.)

McLEOD, ADDISON.

Plays and Players of Modern Italy. Sergel, 1912. ($2.75.)

MATTHEWS, BRANDER.

French Dramatists of the Nineteenth Century. Scribner, 1906. ($1.25.)

MODERWELL, HIRAM KELLY.

The Theater of To-day. Lane, 1914. ($1.50.)

PALMER, JOHN.

The Future of the Theater. Bell, London, 1913.

POLLARD, PERCIVAL.

Masks and Minstrels of New Germany. Luce, 1911. ($1.50.)

Scott, Clement.

> The Drama of Yesterday and To-day. Macmillan, 1899.

Witkowski, Georg.

> The German Drama of the Nineteenth Century. Holt, 1909. ($1.00.)

For further bibliography as well as general history, see Encyclopedia Britannica, 11th edition, article "Drama," and for special bibliography on the Theater and on particular writers, see "The Index of Bibliography," published by the Boston Book Co., Boston.

III. Collected dramatic criticism:

Archer, William.

> The Theatrical World. (5 vols.) Walter Scott, London, 1893-7.

Eaton, Walter Prichard.

> The American Stage of To-day. Small, Maynard, 1908. ($1.50.)

> At the New Theatre and Others. Small, Maynard, 1910. ($1.50.)

Grein, J. T.

> Dramatic Criticism. John Long, London, 1899.

> Premières of the Year. Macqueen, London, 1900.

> Dramatic Criticism. Greening, London, 1901.

> Dramatic Criticism. Evelyn Nash, London, 1904.

Hapgood, Norman.

> The Stage in America 1899-1900. Macmillan, 1901. ($1.75.)

MONTAGUE, C. E.
   Dramatic Values. Macmillan, 1911. ($1.25.)
NIRDLINGER, CHARLES FREDERICK.
   Masques and Mummers. DeWitt, 1899.
SHAW, GEORGE BERNARD.
   Dramatic Opinions and Essays. (2 vols.)
      Brentano, 1906. ($2.50.)
WALBROOK, H. M.
   Nights at the Play. W. J. Ham-Smith, London,
      1911.
WALKLEY, A. B.
   The Drama and Life. Brentano, London, 1911.
      ($1.75.)
   Frames of Mind. Grant Richards, London,
      1899.

INDEX

239

ARCHIBALD HENDERSON'S THE CHANGING DRAMA

Its Contributions and Tendencies. By the Author of "George Bernard Shaw: His Life and Works," "European Dramatists," etc. 12mo. $1.50 net.

The pioneer book in English in its field. While a number of good books, taking up important dramatists and discussing them one after another, are available, this is probably the first that describes the significant changes and movements in the drama of the last half century, illustrating them by the work of leading dramatists and by apt citations of and quotations from their plays. The author, publicist as well as dramatic critic, aims to show the expression of the larger realities of contemporary life in the drama, the widening of social influence of the stage, the new technic, form, and content of the play, the substitution of the theme for the hero, the conflict of wills for that of arms, etc. In short, to give a brief but authoritative general survey with a more detailed appraisal of some of the chief creative contributions.

The chapter headings indicate the content and scope of the work: Drama in the New Age; The New Criticism and New Ethics; Science and the New Drama; The New Forms—Realism and the Pulpit Stage; The New Forms—Naturalism and the Free Theatre; The Battle with Illusions; The Ancient Bondage and the New Freedom; The New Technic; The Play and the Reader; The New Content; The Newer Tendencies.

The author, though an American, has also studied the drama in the theatres of Great Britain and the Continent, and has before this demonstrated that he is a dramatic scholar and a keen, clear-eyed, entertaining critic. His articles have appeared in *La Société Nouvelle, Mercure de France, Deutsche Revue, Illustreret Tidende, Finsk Tidskrift, T. P.'s Magazine,* etc., etc.

Maurice Maeterlinck said of his "Interpreters of Life" (now incorporated in his "European Dramatists"): "You have written one of the most sagacious, most acute, and most penetrating essays in the whole modern literary movement."

"It is a really great work," said Professor William Lyon Phelps of "George Bernard Shaw: His Life and Works."

Of his "European Dramatists," *The Dial* said: "The criticisms of their work are keen and lucid, and have the advantage of coming from one who has studied the plays exhaustively."

HENRY HOLT AND COMPANY
PUBLISHERS   vii'14   NEW YORK

PLAYS

Richard Burton's RAHAB. A drama of the fall of Jericho (in verse.) Illustrated. $1.25 net.

Beulah Marie Dix's ALLISON'S LAD, *The Hundreth Trick, The Weakest Link, The Snare and the Fowler, The Captain of the Gate, The Dark of the Dawn.* One act Martial Interludes. $1.35 net.

Michael Field's CALLIRRHOE; FAIR ROSAMUND. (Dramas in verse.) $1.25.

Henrik Hertz's KING RENE'S DAUGHTER. (A drama in verse.) $1.25.

Kalidasa's SHAKUNTALA. Translated by Prof. A. H. Edgren. $1.50.

Lessing's NATHAN THE WISE. Translated by Ellen Frothingham. $1.50.

Geo. Middleton's EMBERS, with *The Failures, In His House, The Gargoyle, Madonna, The Man Masterful.* $1.35 net.

George Middleton's TRADITION. With *On Bail, Waiting, Their Wife, Mothers, The Cheat of Pity.* Another volume of one act plays of *American Life.* $1.35 net.

Chas. Leonard Moore's THE BANQUET OF PALACIOS. A comedy of South America. To-day. $1.00.

Martin Schutze's HERO AND LEANDER. A tragedy in verse. $1.25 net.

Martin Schutze's JUDITH. A tragedy in verse $1.25 net.

Margaret L. Woods' THE PRINCESS OF HANOVER. An historical tragedy in verse. $1.50.

*₊*For a large number of plays in Foreign Languages, see the publishers' FOREIGN LANGUAGE CATALOG.

PLAYS FOR YOUNG FOLKS

Constance D'Arcy Mackay's PATRIOTIC PLAYS AND PAGEANTS, *Pageant of Patriotism, Hawthorne Pageant.* Parts of the first pageant can be given as one act plays. $1.35 net.

C. D'A. Mackay's THE HOUSE OF THE HEART with *The Enchanted Garden, A Little Pilgrim's Progress, A Pageant of Hours, On Christmas Eve, The Elf Child, The Princess and the Pixies,* etc. $1.10 net.

C. D'A. Mackay's THE SILVER THREAD and other Folk Plays, including *The Forest Spring, Troll Magic, The Three Wishes, Siegfried, The Snow Witch,* etc. $1.10 net.

*** For a number of French and German plays for young folk, see also the publishers' FOREIGN LANGUAGE CATALOG.

Postage on net books 8% additional.

HENRY HOLT AND COMPANY
34 WEST 33d STREET   NEW YORK

THE THEATRE

Clayton Hamilton's THEORY OF THE THEATRE. $1.50 net.

Edward Everett Hale, Jr.'s DRAMATISTS OF TO-DAY. Rostand, Hauptmann, Sudermann, Pinero, Shaw, Phillips, Maeterlinck. New Edition with Portraits. $1.50 net.

George Witkowski's GERMAN DRAMA OF THE NINETEENTH CENTURY. $1.00 net.

Calvin Thomas's LIFE AND WORKS OF SCHILLER. $1.50 net.

W. Fraser Rae's LIFE OF RICHARD BRINSLEY SHERIDAN. With portraits. 2 vols. $7.00.

Jerome K. Jerome's ON THE STAGE—AND OFF. Humorous articles on *The Hero, The Stage Child, The Villain* and other stage types. Illustrated. $1.00.

Eva Lathbury's THE SINKING SHIP. A novel of London Theatrical Life, To-day. $1.50.

SHAKESPEARE

Bernhard ten Brink's FIVE LECTURES ON SHAKESPEARE. *The Poet and the Man, The Chronology of Shakepeare's Works, Shakespeare as Dramatist, Shakespeare as Comic Poet, Shakespeare as Tragic Writer.* Index to works mentioned. Translated by Julia Franklin. $1.25 net.

Stopford Brooke's ON TEN PLAYS OF SHAKESPEARE. *Midsummer Night's Dream, Romeo and Juliet, Richard I, Richard II, Merchant of Venice, As You Like It, Macbeth, Coriolanus, Winter's Tale, The Tempest.* $2.25 net.

Stopford Brooke's ON TEN FURTHER PLAYS OF SHAKESPEARE. *Much Ado About Nothing, Twelfth Night, Julius Caesar, Hamlet, Measure for Measure, Othello, King John, King Lear, Henry IV (1, 2); Henry V.* Probable price, $2.25 net. (May.)

John Masefield's SHAKESPEARE. (Home University Library.) 50c. net.

Charlton M. Lewis's THE GENESIS OF HAMLET. $1.25 net.

Felix E. Schelling's ENGLISH LITERATURE DURING THE LIFETIME OF SHAKESPEARE. $2.50 net.

Henry Thew. Stephenson's SHAKESPEARE'S LONDON. Illustrated. $2.00 net.

Stephenson's THE ELIZABETHAN PEOPLE.. Illustrated. $2.00 net.

Postage on net books 8% additional

HENRY HOLT AND COMPANY
PUBLISHERS   NEW YORK

A FEW RECENT PLAYS BY AMERICANS

Beulah M. Dix's ACROSS THE BORDER

A play against war, showing in four scenes, two "beyond the border" of life, the adventures of a highly likable young Lieutenant. He goes on a desperate mission, finds The Place of Quiet and The Dream Girl, as well as The Place of Winds, where he learns the real nature of War, and finally in a field hospital tries to deliver his message. With 2 illustrations, 80 cents net.

New York Tribune: "One of the few pleas for peace that touch both the heart and the intelligence. . . . Its remarkable blending of stark realism with extravagant fancy strikes home. . . . It is well nigh impossible to rid one's mind of its stirring effect."

New York Times: "Impressive, elaborate and ambitious. . . . A voice raised in the theater against the monstrous horror and infamy of war. . . . The Junior Lieutenant has in him just a touch of 'The Brushwood Boy.'"

Of the author's "ALLISON'S LAD" and other one-act plays of various wars ($1.35 net), *The Transcript* said, "The technical mastery of Miss Dix is great, but her spiritual mastery is greater. For this book lives in the memory."

Percival L. Wilde's DAWN and Other One-Act Plays

"Short, sharp and decisive" episodes of contemporary life. Notable for force, interest and at times humor. $1.20 net.

DAWN, a tense episode in the hut of a brutal miner, with a supernatural climax. THE NOBLE LORD, a comedy about a lady, who angled with herself as bait. THE TRAITOR is discovered by a ruse of a British commanding officer. A HOUSE OF CARDS, about a closed door, and what was on the other side—tragic. PLAYING WITH FIRE, a comedy about the devotion of a boy and girl. THE FINGER OF GOD points the way to an ex-criminal by means of a girl he had never seen before.

Lily A. Long's RADISSON: *The Voyageur*

A highly picturesque play in four acts and in verse. The central figures are Radisson the redoubtable voyageur who explored the Upper Mississippi, his brother-in-law Groseilliers, Owera the daughter of an Indian chief, and various other Indians. The daring resource of the two white men in the face of imminent peril, the pathetic love of Owera, and above all, the vivid pictures of Indian life, the women grinding corn, the council, dances, feasting and famine are notable features, and over it all is a somewhat unusual feeling for the moods of nature which closely follow those of the people involved. $1.00 net.

HENRY HOLT AND COMPANY
PUBLISHERS   NEW YORK

BOOKS ON AND OF SCHOOL PLAYS

By Constance D'Arcy Mackay

HOW TO PRODUCE CHILDREN'S PLAYS

The author is a recognized authority on the production of plays and pageants in the public schools, and combines enthusiastic sympathy with sound, practical instructions. She tells both how to inspire and care for the young actor, how to make costumes, properties, scenery, where to find designs for them, what music to use, etc., etc. She prefaces it all with an interesting historical sketch of the plays-for-children movement, includes elaborate detailed analyses of performances of Browning's *Pied Piper* and Rosetti's *Pageant of the Months,* and concludes with numerous valuable analytical lists of plays for various grades and occasions. $1.20 net (Feb., 1914).

PATRIOTIC PLAYS AND PAGEANTS

PAGEANT OF PATRIOTISM (Outdoor and Indoor Versions):— *Princess Pocahontas, Pilgrim Interlude, Ferry Farm Episode, *George Washington's Fortune, *Daniel Boone: Patriot, Benjamin Franklin Episode, Lincoln Episode, Final Tableau.

HAWTHORNE PAGEANT (for Outdoor or Indoor Production):—Chorus of Spirits of the Old Manse, Prologue by the Muse of Hawthorne, In Witchcraft Days, Dance Interlude, Merrymount, etc.

The portions marked with a star (*) are one-act plays suitable for separate performance. There are full directions for simple costumes, scenes, and staging. 12mo. $1.35 net.

THE HOUSE OF THE HEART

Short plays in verse for children of fourteen or younger:— "The House of the Heart (Morality Play)—"The Enchanted Garden" (Flower Play)—"A Little Pilgrim's Progress" (Morality Play)—"A Pageant of Hours" (To be given Out of Doors)—"On Christmas Eve." "The Princess and the Pixies." "The Christmas Guest" (Miracle Play.), etc. $1.10 net.

"An addition to child drama which has been sorely needed."—*Boston Transcript.*

THE SILVER THREAD

AND OTHER FOLK PLAYS. "The Silver Thread" (Cornish); he Forest Spring" (Italian); "The Foam Maiden" (Celtic); oll Magic" (Norwegian); "The Three Wishes" (French); Brewing of Brains" (English); "Siegfried" (German); Snow Witch" (Russian). $1.10 net.

NRY HOLT AND COMPANY

HERS   NEW YORK